Basic Computation Series 2

Quizzes and Tests

MW01139861

Loretta M. Taylor, Ed. D.

Harold D. Taylor, Ed. D.

Dale Seymour Publications®
Parsippany, New Jersey

Executive Editor: Catherine Anderson

Editorial Manager: Carolyn Coyle

Development Editor: Deborah J. Slade

Production/Manufacturing Director: Janet Yearian

Sr. Production/Manufacturing Coordinator: Roxanne Knoll

Art Director: Jim O'Shea

Design Manager: Jeff Kelly

Cover Designer: Monika Popowitz

Interior Designer: Christy Butterfield

Dale Seymour Publications
An imprint of Pearson Learning
299 Jefferson Road
Parsippany, NJ 07054-0480
www.pearsonlearning.com
Customer Service: 1-800-321-3106

ISBN 0-7690-0123-8

1 2 3 4 5 6 7 8 9 10–ML–03 02 01 00 99

This Book Is Printed
On Recycled Paper

Authors of the Basic Computation Series 2000

Loretta M. Taylor is a retired high school mathematics teacher. During her teaching career, she taught at Hillsdale High School in San Mateo, California; Crestmoor High School in San Bruno, California; Patterson High School in Patterson, California; Round Valley Union High School in Covelo, California; and Farmington High School in Farmington, New Mexico. Dr. Taylor obtained a B.S. in mathematics from Southeastern Oklahoma State University, and both an M.A. in mathematics and an Ed.D. in mathematics education from the University of Northern Colorado. She has been active in professional organizations at the local, state, and national levels, including the National Council of Teachers of Mathematics, the California Mathematics Council, the National Education Association, and the California Teachers Association. She has given a variety of talks and workshops at numerous conferences, schools, and univėrsities. Dr. Taylor is a member of Lambda Sigma Tau, a national honorary science fraternity, and is coauthor of *Paper and Scissors Polygons and More, Algebra Book 1, Algebra Book 2,* and *Developing Skills in Algebra 1.* In retirement, she continues to be an active mathematics author and is involved with community organizations.

Harold D. Taylor is a retired high school mathematics teacher, having taught at Aragon High School in San Mateo, California; as well as at Patterson High School in Patterson, California; Round Valley Union High School in Covelo, California; and Farmington High School in Farmington, New Mexico. He has served in high schools not only as a mathematics teacher, but also as a mathematics department head and as an assistant principal. He received a B.S. in mathematics from Southeastern Oklahoma State University, and both an M.A. in mathematics and an Ed.D. in mathematics education from the University of Northern Colorado. Dr. Taylor has been very active in a number of professional organizations, having worked in a variety of significant capacities for the National Council of Teachers of Mathematics and the California Mathematics Council. He was chairman of the Publicity and Information Committee and the Local Organizing Committee for the Fourth International Congress on Mathematics Education at Berkeley, California, was on the writing team of the California Assessment Test, and was a member of the California State Mathematics Framework and Criteria Committee, chairing the California State Mathematics Framework Addendum Committee. Since 1966, he has spoken at more than one hundred local, state, and national meetings on mathematics and mathematics education. Dr. Taylor is author of *Ten Mathematics Projects and Career Education Infusion,* and coauthor of *Algebra Book 1, Algebra Book 2,* and *Developing Skills in Algebra 1.* In 1989 he was the California recipient of the Presidential Award for Excellence in Teaching Secondary Mathematics. In retirement, Dr. Taylor is continuing to produce mathematics materials for the classroom, and also serves his community as County Judge in Custer County, Colorado, having been appointed to this position by Governor Roy Romer.

Table of Contents

Tests

A Note of Introduction

To the Teacher

Some students are familiar with computational work but have never really mastered it. Perhaps this is a result of a lack of practice. With the *Basic Computation Series 2000,* you can provide students with as much practice as they need. You can teach, check up, reteach, and reinforce. You can give classwork and homework. If you wish, you can create a full year's course in basic computation, or you can provide skills maintenance when it's needed. All the work is here. Select the pages you want to use for the students who need them.

To the Student

You can't play a guitar before you learn the chords. You can't shoot a hook shot before you learn the layup. You can't pass a mathematics exam before you learn to compute, and you can't master computational skills until you learn the mathematical facts and procedures. Learning takes practice; there are no shortcuts. The pages in this book are for practice. Do your math every day and think about what you're doing. If you don't understand something, ask questions. Don't do too much work in your head; it's worth an extra sheet of paper to write down your steps. Also, be patient with yourself. Learning takes time.

Although calculators and other computational devices are readily available to most everyone, you will be forever handicapped if you are not able to perform basic mathematical computations without the aid of a mechanical or electronic computational device. Learn and master the procedures so that you can rely on your own abilities.

To the Parent

The importance of the development of mathematical skills cannot be emphasized enough. Mathematics is needed to estimate materials for a construction job or to price a car. It's needed to predict earthquakes and to prescribe medicine. It helps you determine how to stretch your dollars and pay your bills. This program provides the practice students need to develop the essential computational skills. Conventional algorithms are utilized throughout the *Basic Computation Series 2000.* You can help your children learn these skills. Give them your support and encouragement. Urge them to do their homework. Be there to answer their questions. Give them a quiet place to work. Make them feel good about trying. Your help can make the difference.

About the Program

What is the Basic Computation Series 2000?

The books in the *Basic Computation Series 2000* provide comprehensive practice on all the essential computational skills. There are nine practice books and a test book. The practice books consist of carefully sequenced drill worksheets organized in groups of five. The test book contains daily quizzes (160 quizzes in all), semester tests, and year-end tests written in standardized-test format.

Book 1	Working with Whole Numbers
Book 2	Understanding Fractions
Book 3	Working with Fractions
Book 4	Working with Decimals
Book 5	Working with Percents
Book 6	Understanding Measurement
Book 7	Working with Perimeter and Area
Book 8	Working with Surface Area and Volume
Book 9	Applying Computational Skills
Test Book 10	Basic Computation Quizzes and Tests

Who can use the Basic Computation Series 2000?

The *Basic Computation Series 2000* is appropriate for use by any person, young or old, who has not achieved computational proficiency. It may be used with any program calling for carefully sequenced computational practice. The material is especially suitable for use with students in fifth grade, middle school, junior high school, special education classes, and high school. It may be used by classroom teachers, substitute teachers, tutors, and parents. It is also useful for those in adult education, for those preparing for the General Education Development Test (GED), and for others wishing to study on their own.

What is in this book?

This book is a test book. In addition to these teacher notes, it contains quizzes, two first-semester tests, two year-end tests, answers, and a response form.

Quizzes

The quizzes are designed to give teachers the opportunity to check up on students' skills. Each quiz comes in four equivalent forms allowing for four daily quizzes a week. There are 40 weeks of quizzes, 160 quizzes in all. Each quiz provides exercises in only one or two specific skills. Instructions are clear and simple. There are enough problems to give teachers the opportunity to diagnose student errors and few enough for the quizzes to take only a short period of time. The answer to each problem is included in the back of the book.

Tests

The tests provide questions on all the essential computational skills measured on competency tests. There are two 100-question first-semester tests and two 100-question year-end tests, all written in standard multiple-choice format. The tests can be used as final exams for each semester, as practice for final exams, or as practice for minimal competency tests. The answer to each problem is included in the back of the book.

Response Form

A response form similiar to those used with standardized tests is provided for use with the tests.

Answers

Answers to all problems are included in the back of the book.

How can the Basic Computation Series 2000 be used?

The materials in the *Basic Computation Series 2000* can serve as the major skeleton of a skills program or as supplements to any other computational skills program. The large number of worksheets provides a wide variety from which to choose and allows flexibility in structuring a program to meet individual needs. The following suggestions are offered to show how the *Basic Computation Series 2000* may be adapted to a particular situation.

Minimal Competency Practice

In various fields and schools, standardized tests are used for entrance, passage from one level to another, and certification of competency or proficiency prior to graduation. The materials in the *Basic Computation Series 2000* are particularly well-suited to preparing for any of the various mathematics competency tests, including the mathematics portion of the General Education Development Test (GED) used to certify high school equivalency.

Together, the books in the *Basic Computation Series 2000* provide practice on all the essential computational skills. The worksheets can be used to brush up on skills measured by competency tests. The quizzes can be used to check up on previously-studied skills. The semester tests and year-end tests are written in standardized-test format and can be used as sample minimal competency tests.

Skills Maintenance

The quizzes come in four equivalent forms, allowing for daily maintenance of previously-learned skills and diagnosis of skill deficiencies. Used along with the daily worksheets from the other books in the *Basic Computation Series 2000,* they provide either warm-up or check-up activities for each day's work. The tests can be used at the end of each semester to assess proficiency. Since there are two forms of each test, one form could be used for review and practice, and the other form for the examination.

Supplementary Drill

There are more than 18,000 problems in the *Basic Computation Series 2000*. When students need more practice with a given skill, use the appropriate worksheets from the series. They are suitable for classwork or homework practice following the teaching of a specific skill. With five equivalent pages for most worksheets, adequate practice is provided for each essential skill.

How are the materials prepared?

The books are designed with pages that can be easily reproduced. Permanent transparencies can be produced using a copy machine and special transparencies designed for this purpose. The program will run more smoothly if the student's work is stored in folders. Record sheets can be attached to the folders so that students, teachers, or parents can keep records of an individual's progress. Materials stored in this way are readily available for conferences with the student or parent.

Addition of Whole Numbers

Find each sum.

1.   5
     3
     6
     9
  + 8
	2. 423,987
	  + 27,854
		3. Find the sum of 9, 58, and 725.

4.   15
    79
     3
  874
  + 72
	5. 73
	    57
	    49
	  + 21
		6. $29 + 83 + 47 = ?$

7. Find the sum of 387, 425, and 478.	**8.** $49 + 1{,}302 + 84 = ?$	**9.** 876
		    14,247
		      900
		 + 7,003,468

10. 5,473
    439
  6,347
 + 246
	11. Find the sum of 27,867 and 946.	**12.** 7,395,460
		    672,008
		 + 45,538,475

13. Find the sum of 407,083, 39, and 575.	**14.** 10,457
	  206,003
	     290
	   4,580
	 + 72,342
		15. $561 + 27 + 303 = ?$

Addition of Whole Numbers

Find each sum.

1. 6 5 9 4 + 7	**2.** 637,495 + 46,887	**3.** Find the sum of 7, 95, and 823.
4. 15 72 8 946 + 74	**5.** 73 75 46 29 + 37	**6.** $25 + 73 + 48 = ?$
7. Find the sum of 583, 217, and 423.	**8.** $43 + 1,506 + 96 = ?$	**9.** 875 14,372 900 + 700,893
10. 4,396 297 8,625 + 263	**11.** Find the sum of 37,854 and 972.	**12.** 8,395,680 748,005 + 41,568,337
13. Find the sum of 506,842, 73, and 592.	**14.** 10,638 307,004 297 4,845 + 57,250	**15.** $472 + 27 + 506 = ?$

Addition of Whole Numbers

Find each sum.

1.   5
      7
      9
      3
 + 8
	2. 538,427
	 + 95,374
		3. Find the sum of 8, 47, and 764.

4.   18
     63
      9
   431
 +   87
	5. 93
	     65
	     82
	     43
	 + 52
		6. $46 + 82 + 73 = ?$

7. Find the sum of 272, 583, and 921.	**8.** $62 + 1{,}307 + 48 = ?$	**9.** 672
		   23,557
		     800
		 + 800,853

10.   3,827
     934
   5,956
 +   732
	11. Find the sum of 43,781 and 856.	**12.** 8,976,314
		    825,503
		 + 68,843,705

13. Find the sum of 807,463, 29, and 482.	**14.** 20,533
	   609,004
	      368
	    6,965
	 + 38,544
		15. $352 + 72 + 804 = ?$

Addition of Whole Numbers

Find each sum.

1. 9 8 7 2 + 4	**2.** 384,762 + 58,773	**3.** Find the sum of 7, 64, and 823.
4. 26 93 8 772 + 83	**5.** 54 47 63 + 51	**6.** $38 + 52 + 69 = ?$
7. Find the sum of 548, 821, and 694.	**8.** $86 + 1,407 + 92 = ?$	**9.** 436 15,762 800 + 8,005,937
10. 8,327 631 5,357 + 462	**11.** Find the sum of 59,473 and 968.	**12.** 8,359,281 697,006 + 59,463,227
13. Find the sum of 907,035, 53, and 281.	**14.** 20,674 357,963 340 3,690 + 58,731	**15.** $895 + 36 + 404 = ?$

Basic Computation Series 2000: Quizzes and Tests

Subtraction of Whole Numbers

Find each difference.

1. $\begin{array}{r} 469 \\ -\ \ 95 \\ \hline \end{array}$	**2.** $486 - 85 = ?$	**3.** $\begin{array}{r} 71{,}003 \\ -\ 1{,}596 \\ \hline \end{array}$
4. Find the difference between 5,837 and 712.	**5.** $\begin{array}{r} 8{,}854 \\ -\ \ 895 \\ \hline \end{array}$	**6.** Subtract 94 from 736.
7. What number is 41 less than 600?	**8.** $575 - 136 = ?$	**9.** Find the difference between 583 and 795.
10. $15{,}876 - 12{,}482 = ?$	**11.** $\begin{array}{r} 50{,}903 \\ -\ 4{,}726 \\ \hline \end{array}$	**12.** $\begin{array}{r} 813{,}230 \\ -\ 97{,}538 \\ \hline \end{array}$
13. 7,132 is how much more than 3,567?	**14.** Subtract 436 from 862.	**15.** $703{,}624 - 999 = ?$

Subtraction of Whole Numbers

Find each difference.

1. 694 − 372	**2.** 268 − 94 = ?	**3.** 46,993 − 735
4. Find the difference between 974 and 385.	**5.** 45,139 − 8,457	**6.** Subtract 63 from 97.
7. Subtract 247 from 314.	**8.** 274 − 75 = ?	**9.** Find the difference between 549 and 827.
10. 69,470 − 398	**11.** 90,048 − 6,095	**12.** 493,094 − 38,245
13. 2,793 is how much more than 2,489?	**14.** Subtract 394 from 2,356.	**15.** 540,027 − 595 = ?

Subtraction of Whole Numbers

Find each difference.

1. 87,463 − 6,292	**2.** Subtract 6,389 from 7,499.	**3.** 43,521 − 37,483 = ?
4. Subtract 478 from 15,620.	**5.** 55,555 − 39,586	**6.** 972 − 499 = ?
7. Subtract 15,791 from 24,650.	**8.** 75,643 − 9,822 = ?	**9.** Subtract 1,668 from 3,577.
10. 12,345 − 6,789	**11.** 25,371 − 19,850 = ?	**12.** Subtract 3,333 from 12,121.
13. Subtract 189 from 240.	**14.** 53,520 − 47,631	**15.** 50,403 − 3,624 = ?

Subtraction of Whole Numbers

Find each difference.

1. 69,235 − 8,316	**2.** Subtract 9,325 from 18,330.	**3.** 92,351 − 26,538 = ?
4. Subtract 947 from 26,830.	**5.** 66,666 − 48,789	**6.** 887 − 388 = ?
7. Subtract 35,612 from 57,431.	**8.** 13,976 − 8,732 = ?	**9.** Subtract 1,792 from 4,699.
10. 31,426 − 7,839	**11.** 35,816 − 13,720 = ?	**12.** Subtract 2,222 from 31,313.
13. Subtract 159 from 360.	**14.** 73,750 − 56,241	**15.** 60,702 − 4,634 = ?

Basic Computation Series 2000: Quizzes and Tests

Multiplication by One-Digit Numbers

Find each product.

1. $\begin{array}{r} 27 \\ \times\ 1 \\ \hline \end{array}$	**2.** $\begin{array}{r} 98 \\ \times\ 4 \\ \hline \end{array}$	**3.** $\begin{array}{r} 69 \\ \times\ 5 \\ \hline \end{array}$
4. $\begin{array}{r} 20 \\ \times\ 7 \\ \hline \end{array}$	**5.** $\begin{array}{r} 36 \\ \times\ 9 \\ \hline \end{array}$	**6.** $\begin{array}{r} 35 \\ \times\ 8 \\ \hline \end{array}$
7. $\begin{array}{r} 15 \\ \times\ 7 \\ \hline \end{array}$	**8.** $\begin{array}{r} 67 \\ \times\ 9 \\ \hline \end{array}$	**9.** $\begin{array}{r} 53 \\ \times\ 7 \\ \hline \end{array}$
10. $\begin{array}{r} 860 \\ \times\ 9 \\ \hline \end{array}$	**11.** $\begin{array}{r} 571 \\ \times\ 9 \\ \hline \end{array}$	**12.** $\begin{array}{r} 136 \\ \times\ 6 \\ \hline \end{array}$

Multiplication by One-Digit Numbers

Find each product.

1. 51 × 2	**2.** 40 × 4	**3.** 29 × 1
4. 54 × 6	**5.** 98 × 3	**6.** 36 × 5
7. 40 × 2	**8.** 81 × 3	**9.** 49 × 6
10. 153 × 9	**11.** 267 × 8	**12.** 348 × 7

Multiplication by One-Digit Numbers

Find each product.

1. 15 $\times$ 3	**2.** 24 $\times$ 5	**3.** 18 $\times$ 6
4. 36 $\times$ 7	**5.** 47 $\times$ 8	**6.** 29 $\times$ 9
7. 739 $\times$ 3	**8.** 587 $\times$ 9	**9.** 138 $\times$ 6
10. 597 $\times$ 5	**11.** 843 $\times$ 7	**12.** 1,436 $\times$ 8

Multiplication by One-Digit Numbers

Find each product.

1. 12 $\times$ 7	**2.** 342 $\times$ 8	**3.** 783 $\times$ 4
4. 596 $\times$ 3	**5.** 843 $\times$ 5	**6.** 1,396 $\times$ 6
7. 348 $\times$ 2	**8.** 513 $\times$ 9	**9.** 524 $\times$ 8
10. 678 $\times$ 3	**11.** 403 $\times$ 4	**12.** 589 $\times$ 1

Multiplication by Two-Digit Numbers

Find each product.

1.   15
   × 12
	2. 24
	   × 35
		3. 10
		   × 16

4.   84
   × 47
	5. 98
	   × 15
		6. 44
		   × 89

7.   129
   × 10
	8. 293
	   × 23
		9. 402
		   × 67

10.   276
   × 45
	11. 345
	   × 81
		12. 782
		   × 96

Multiplication by Two-Digit Numbers

Find each product.

1. $\begin{array}{r} 17 \\ \times\ 35 \end{array}$	2. $\begin{array}{r} 18 \\ \times\ 40 \end{array}$	3. $\begin{array}{r} 76 \\ \times\ 29 \end{array}$
4. $\begin{array}{r} 84 \\ \times\ 37 \end{array}$	5. $\begin{array}{r} 20 \\ \times\ 16 \end{array}$	6. $\begin{array}{r} 59 \\ \times\ 31 \end{array}$
7. $\begin{array}{r} 462 \\ \times\ 38 \end{array}$	8. $\begin{array}{r} 79 \\ \times\ 52 \end{array}$	9. $\begin{array}{r} 146 \\ \times\ 85 \end{array}$
10. $\begin{array}{r} 237 \\ \times\ 91 \end{array}$	11. $\begin{array}{r} 420 \\ \times\ 64 \end{array}$	12. $\begin{array}{r} 508 \\ \times\ 83 \end{array}$

Multiplication by Two-Digit Numbers

Find each product.

1. 43 $\times$ 25	**2.** 16 $\times$ 70	**3.** 89 $\times$ 26
4. 57 $\times$ 13	**5.** 48 $\times$ 91	**6.** 40 $\times$ 13
7. 253 $\times$ 36	**8.** 348 $\times$ 94	**9.** 149 $\times$ 38
10. 256 $\times$ 73	**11.** 407 $\times$ 98	**12.** 126 $\times$ 35

NAME _____　　　　DATE _____

Multiplication by Two-Digit Numbers

Find each product.

1. 47 $\times$ 20	**2.** 26 $\times$ 18	**3.** 20 $\times$ 45
4. 26 $\times$ 34	**5.** 75 $\times$ 93	**6.** 82 $\times$ 15
7. 618 $\times$ 55	**8.** 523 $\times$ 72	**9.** 734 $\times$ 93
10. 256 $\times$ 60	**11.** 728 $\times$ 29	**12.** 375 $\times$ 71

NAME _____

DATE _____

Multiplication of Whole Numbers

Find each product.

1.   2,705
    ×   9
	2. Multiply 47 by 76.	**3.** 7,334
		    × 35

4. 39 × 54 = ?	**5.** 243 × 307	**6.** Find the product of 73 and 28.
7. 37 × 12 × 4 = ?	**8.** Multiply 89 by 137.	**9.** 43 × 11 × 0 = ?
10. 76 × 9 = ?	**11.** 3,007 × 280	**12.** Find the product of 17 and 23.

Multiplication of Whole Numbers

Find each product.

1. 3,476 $\times$ 27	**2.** Multiply 93 by 48.	**3.** 9,999 $\times$ 406
4. 68 $\times$ 27 = ?	**5.** 176 $\times$ 437	**6.** Find the product of 37 and 89.
7. 16 $\times$ 27 $\times$ 11 = ?	**8.** 4,009 $\times$ 273	**9.** 19 $\times$ 57 = ?
10. 15 $\times$ 25 = ?	**11.** 17 $\times$ 23 $\times$ 4 = ?	**12.** Find the product of 14 and 12.

Basic Computation Series 2000: Quizzes and Tests

Multiplication of Whole Numbers

Find each product.

1.   7,382
   $\times$ 8
	2. Multiply 83 by 27.	**3.** 5,863
		   $\times$ 45

4. $37 \times 63 = ?$	**5.** 407 $\times$ 20	**6.** Find the product of 137 and 14.
7. $43 \times 35 \times$		**9.** $85 \times 0 \times 592 = ?$
10. $55 \times 7 = ?$	**11.** 5,072 $\times$ 630	**12.** Find the product of 24 and 16.

Multiplication of Whole Numbers

Find each product.

1. $\begin{array}{r} 6{,}922 \\ \times \quad 8 \\ \hline \end{array}$	**2.** Multiply 39 by 14.	**3.** $\begin{array}{r} 5{,}607 \\ \times \quad 67 \\ \hline \end{array}$
4. $59 \times 37 = ?$	**5.** $\begin{array}{r} 702 \\ \times \ 601 \\ \hline \end{array}$	**6.** Find the product of 92 and 46.
7. $17 \times 28 \times 3 = ?$	**8.** Multiply 37 by 2,745.	**9.** $0 \times 62 \times 71 = ?$
10. $427 \times 8 = ?$	**11.** $\begin{array}{r} 8{,}025 \\ \times \ 314 \\ \hline \end{array}$	**12.** Find the product of 42 and 18.

Basic Computation Series 2000: Quizzes and Tests

Division by One-Digit Numbers

Find each quotient.

1. 63 ÷ 7 = ?	**2.** 48 ÷ 8 = ?	**3.** 35 ÷ 5 = ?
4. 0 ÷ 5 = ?	**5.** 8 ÷ 1 = ?	**6.** 24 ÷ 3 = ?
7. 54 ÷ 6 = ?	**8.** 56 ÷ 7 = ?	**9.** 42 ÷ 6 = ?
10. 25 ÷ 5 = ?	**11.** 21 ÷ 7 = ?	**12.** 21 ÷ 3 = ?
13. 50 ÷ 5 = ?	**14.** 72 ÷ 9 = ?	**15.** 81 ÷ 9 = ?
16. 30 ÷ 6 = ?	**17.** 28 ÷ 7 = ?	**18.** 40 ÷ 8 = ?
19. 27 ÷ 9 = ?	**20.** 60 ÷ 10 = ?	**21.** 100 ÷ 10 = ?
22. 24 ÷ 6 = ?	**23.** 36 ÷ 6 = ?	**24.** 32 ÷ 8 = ?
25. 64 ÷ 8 = ?	**26.** 18 ÷ 3 = ?	**27.** 70 ÷ 10 = ?
28. 20 ÷ 4 = ?	**29.** 0 ÷ 10 = ?	**30.** 18 ÷ 9 = ?

NAME _____   DATE _____

Division by One-Digit Numbers

Find each quotient.

1. $26 \div 3 = ?$	**2.** $17 \div 2 = ?$	**3.** $29 \div 4 = ?$
4. $58 \div 7 = ?$	**5.** $11 \div 2 = ?$	**6.** $31 \div 4 = ?$
7. $23 \div 4 = ?$	**8.** $20 \div 3 = ?$	**9.** $9 \div 2 = ?$
10. $60 \div 9 = ?$	**11.** $50 \div 8 = ?$	**12.** $33 \div 5 = ?$
13. $39 \div 8 = ?$	**14.** $27 \div 4 = ?$	**15.** $19 \div 3 = ?$
16. $42 \div 5 = ?$	**17.** $56 \div 6 = ?$	**18.** $83 \div 9 = ?$
19. $61 \div 8 = ?$	**20.** $54 \div 7 = ?$	**21.** $32 \div 6 = ?$
22. $43 \div 5 = ?$	**23.** $39 \div 9 = ?$	**24.** $53 \div 8 = ?$
25. $41 \div 4 = ?$	**26.** $57 \div 7 = ?$	**27.** $49 \div 8 = ?$
28. $30 \div 9 = ?$	**29.** $67 \div 8 = ?$	**30.** $19 \div 2 = ?$

Basic Computation Series 2000: Quizzes and Tests

NAME

DATE

Division by One-Digit Numbers

Find each quotient.

1. 7 ÷ 2 = ?	**2.** 14 ÷ 6 = ?	**3.** 29 ÷ 4 = ?
4. 57 ÷ 9 = ?	**5.** 43 ÷ 6 = ?	**6.** 36 ÷ 8 = ?
7. 13 ÷ 2 = ?	**8.** 34 ÷ 6 = ?	**9.** 27 ÷ 4 = ?
10. 45 ÷ 6 = ?	**11.** 36 ÷ 8 = ?	**12.** 38 ÷ 5 = ?
13. 23 ÷ 3 = ?	**14.** 61 ÷ 9 = ?	**15.** 19 ÷ 2 = ?
16. 34 ÷ 7 = ?	**17.** 29 ÷ 9 = ?	**18.** 16 ÷ 3 = ?
19. 53 ÷ 6 = ?	**20.** 51 ÷ 7 = ?	**21.** 23 ÷ 5 = ?
22. 48 ÷ 7 = ?	**23.** 29 ÷ 8 = ?	**24.** 21 ÷ 9 = ?
25. 33 ÷ 4 = ?	**26.** 59 ÷ 4 = ?	**27.** 25 ÷ 3 = ?
28. 15 ÷ 2 = ?	**29.** 17 ÷ 5 = ?	**30.** 29 ÷ 3 = ?

Copyright © Dale Seymour Publications®

Division by One-Digit Numbers

Find each quotient.

1. 39 ÷ 4 = ?	**2.** 60 ÷ 9 = ?	**3.** 56 ÷ 5 = ?
4. 51 ÷ 9 = ?	**5.** 37 ÷ 7 = ?	**6.** 25 ÷ 8 = ?
7. 27 ÷ 7 = ?	**8.** 39 ÷ 7 = ?	**9.** 47 ÷ 8 = ?
10. 28 ÷ 8 = ?	**11.** 43 ÷ 9 = ?	**12.** 45 ÷ 6 = ?
13. 13 ÷ 2 = ?	**14.** 46 ÷ 4 = ?	**15.** 11 ÷ 2 = ?
16. 19 ÷ 6 = ?	**17.** 20 ÷ 8 = ?	**18.** 32 ÷ 5 = ?
19. 17 ÷ 4 = ?	**20.** 20 ÷ 7 = ?	**21.** 16 ÷ 3 = ?
22. 20 ÷ 6 = ?	**23.** 27 ÷ 5 = ?	**24.** 7 ÷ 2 = ?
25. 38 ÷ 5 = ?	**26.** 30 ÷ 7 = ?	**27.** 35 ÷ 6 = ?
28. 44 ÷ 3 = ?	**29.** 60 ÷ 8 = ?	**30.** 17 ÷ 3 = ?

NAME   DATE

Division by Two-Digit Numbers

Find each quotient.

1. $1{,}302 \div 31 = ?$	**2.** $1{,}368 \div 72 = ?$	**3.** $4{,}048 \div 44 = ?$
4. $1{,}971 \div 73 = ?$	**5.** $3{,}904 \div 64 = ?$	**6.** $3{,}649 \div 41 = ?$
7. $2{,}144 \div 32 = ?$	**8.** $1{,}183 \div 13 = ?$	**9.** $4{,}221 \div 63 = ?$
10. $4{,}664 \div 53 = ?$	**11.** $2{,}170 \div 70 = ?$	**12.** $8{,}178 \div 94 = ?$

Division by Two-Digit Numbers

Find each quotient.

1. 924 ÷ 12 = ?	**2.** 5,340 ÷ 60 = ?	**3.** 1,173 ÷ 51 = ?
4. 3,358 ÷ 73 = ?	**5.** 1,248 ÷ 24 = ?	**6.** 6,532 ÷ 92 = ?
7. 1,517 ÷ 41 = ?	**8.** 3,604 ÷ 53 = ?	**9.** 2,241 ÷ 83 = ?
10. 3,200 ÷ 64 = ?	**11.** 5,976 ÷ 72 = ?	**12.** 3,479 ÷ 71 = ?

Division by Two-Digit Numbers

Find each quotient.

1. 3,551 ÷ 53 = ?	**2.** 2,116 ÷ 92 = ?	**3.** 3,478 ÷ 74 = ?
4. 2,916 ÷ 81 = ?	**5.** 4,544 ÷ 64 = ?	**6.** 928 ÷ 32 = ?
7. 1,027 ÷ 13 = ?	**8.** 2,132 ÷ 41 = ?	**9.** 2,697 ÷ 93 = ?
10. 2,508 ÷ 44 = ?	**11.** 3,276 ÷ 52 = ?	**12.** 1,302 ÷ 31 = ?

Division by Two-Digit Numbers

Find each quotient.

1. 4,819 ÷ 61 = ?	**2.** 3,564 ÷ 44 = ?	**3.** 4,232 ÷ 92 = ?
4. 828 ÷ 23 = ?	**5.** 1,728 ÷ 72 = ?	**6.** 1,079 ÷ 13 = ?
7. 2,268 ÷ 54 = ?	**8.** 7,600 ÷ 80 = ?	**9.** 2,738 ÷ 74 = ?
10. 5,208 ÷ 93 = ?	**11.** 756 ÷ 12 = ?	**12.** 600 ÷ 24 = ?

Division by Two-Digit Numbers

Find each quotient.

1. 1,856 ÷ 64 = ?	**2.** 1,908 ÷ 53 = ?	**3.** 1,512 ÷ 21 = ?
4. 5,428 ÷ 92 = ?	**5.** 4,824 ÷ 72 = ?	**6.** 3,483 ÷ 81 = ?
7. 1,118 ÷ 43 = ?	**8.** 510 ÷ 30 = ?	**9.** 812 ÷ 14 = ?
10. 2,870 ÷ 82 = ?	**11.** 4,914 ÷ 63 = ?	**12.** 6,097 ÷ 91 = ?

Division by Two-Digit Numbers

Find each quotient.

1. 414 ÷ 18 = ?	**2.** 782 ÷ 46 = ?	**3.** 928 ÷ 29 = ?
4. 2,993 ÷ 73 = ?	**5.** 1,472 ÷ 16 = ?	**6.** 2,491 ÷ 53 = ?
7. 832 ÷ 26 = ?	**8.** 2,726 ÷ 47 = ?	**9.** 2,745 ÷ 61 = ?
10. 1,456 ÷ 28 = ?	**11.** 2,747 ÷ 67 = ?	**12.** 2,484 ÷ 92 = ?

Basic Computation Series 2000: Quizzes and Tests

Division by Two-Digit Numbers

Find each quotient.

1. 756 ÷ 36 = ?	**2.** 2,544 ÷ 53 = ?	**3.** 594 ÷ 27 = ?
4. 656 ÷ 16 = ?	**5.** 480 ÷ 15 = ?	**6.** 555 ÷ 37 = ?
7. 1,118 ÷ 43 = ?	**8.** 4,524 ÷ 87 = ?	**9.** 462 ÷ 33 = ?
10. 1,550 ÷ 25 = ?	**11.** 1,701 ÷ 63 = ?	**12.** 2,592 ÷ 81 = ?

Division by Two-Digit Numbers

Find each quotient.

1. 1,548 ÷ 36 = ?	**2.** 2,448 ÷ 48 = ?	**3.** 784 ÷ 16 = ?
4. 396 ÷ 18 = ?	**5.** 1,081 ÷ 23 = ?	**6.** 528 ÷ 16 = ?
7. 1,326 ÷ 26 = ?	**8.** 2,112 ÷ 48 = ?	**9.** 1,888 ÷ 59 = ?
10. 2,795 ÷ 65 = ?	**11.** 1,232 ÷ 77 = ?	**12.** 1,911 ÷ 91 = ?

Division of Whole Numbers

Find each quotient.

1. $488 \div 8 = ?$	**2.** Divide 10,472 by 68.	**3.** $304 \div 76 = ?$
4. $7\overline{)336}$	**5.** $9{,}825 \div 75 = ?$	**6.** Divide 392 by 49.
7. $\dfrac{1{,}260}{18} = ?$	**8.** $65\overline{)22{,}555}$	**9.** $30{,}000 \div 100 = ?$
10. $28 \div 4 = ?$	**11.** Divide 600 by 25.	**12.** $2{,}041{,}600 \div 2{,}900 = ?$

Division of Whole Numbers

Find each quotient.

1. 297 ÷ 3 = ?	**2.** Divide 47 into 987.	**3.** Divide 486,234 by 6.
4. $\dfrac{292}{146}$ = ?	**5.** 299 ÷ 13 = ?	**6.** Divide 17,046 by 2,841.
7. Divide 1,488 by 62.	**8.** 882 ÷ 14 = ?	**9.** 1,000 ÷ 10 = ?
10. 119 ÷ 7 = ?	**11.** Divide 169 by 13.	**12.** 1,753,944 ÷ 5,464 = ?

Division of Whole Numbers

Find each quotient.

1. 477 ÷ 9 = ?	**2.** Divide 8,112 by 48.	**3.** 9,612 ÷ 54 = ?
4. $52\overline{)13{,}104}$	**5.** 209,032 ÷ 8 = ?	**6.** 10,000 ÷ 1,000 = ?
7. Divide 43 into 1,763.	**8.** 62,500 ÷ 2,500 = ?	**9.** 13,104 ÷ 52 = ?
10. 279 ÷ 9 = ?	**11.** Divide 235 by 5.	**12.** 16,440,321 ÷ 4,107 = ?

Division of Whole Numbers

Find each quotient.

1. $322 \div 14 = ?$	**2.** Divide 9,922 by 22.	**3.** Divide 42 into 9,198.
4. $35\overline{)2,275}$	**5.** $14,432 \div 41 = ?$	**6.** Divide 4,250 by 125.
7. $49,686 \div 91 = ?$	**8.** $212\overline{)14,628}$	**9.** Divide 141,414 by 14.
10. $81 \div 27 = ?$	**11.** Divide 22,016 by 43.	**12.** $9,200 \div 200 = ?$

Basic Computation Series 2000: Quizzes and Tests

Operations with Whole Numbers

Find each sum, difference, product, or quotient.

1. $\begin{array}{r} 67 \\ 54 \\ 96 \\ 42 \\ + 38 \\ \hline \end{array}$	**2.** $\begin{array}{r} 297{,}012 \\ + 874{,}263 \\ \hline \end{array}$	**3.** $\begin{array}{r} 263 \\ 821 \\ 998 \\ + 516 \\ \hline \end{array}$
4. $\begin{array}{r} 507{,}711 \\ - 89{,}733 \\ \hline \end{array}$	**5.** $\begin{array}{r} 410{,}558 \\ - 273{,}669 \\ \hline \end{array}$	**6.** $\begin{array}{r} 401{,}003 \\ - 272{,}854 \\ \hline \end{array}$
7. $\begin{array}{r} 29 \\ \times 84 \\ \hline \end{array}$	**8.** $\begin{array}{r} 587 \\ \times 375 \\ \hline \end{array}$	**9.** $\begin{array}{r} 509 \\ \times 889 \\ \hline \end{array}$
10. $42\overline{)25{,}746}$	**11.** $803\overline{)452{,}892}$	**12.** $58\overline{)174{,}290}$

Operations with Whole Numbers

Find each sum, difference, product, or quotient.

1. 26 87 95 42 + 23	**2.** 376,214 + 842,615	**3.** 816 759 426 + 115
4. 807,553 − 49,675	**5.** 786,917 − 497,028	**6.** 700,597 − 492,618
7. 67 × 48	**8.** 867 × 385	**9.** 707 × 402
10. 73)66,357	**11.** 711)154,287	**12.** 97)877,268

Operations with Whole Numbers

Find each sum, difference, product, or quotient.

1. 27 62 39 86 + 25	**2.** 784,309 + 873,086	**3.** 721 132 547 + 614
4. 804,712 − 76,538	**5.** 386,207 − 367,319	**6.** 908,043 − 259,476
7. 44 × 29	**8.** 862 × 258	**9.** 705 × 802
10. $27\overline{)2{,}187}$	**11.** $307\overline{)127{,}098}$	**12.** $94\overline{)282{,}470}$

Operations with Whole Numbers

Find each sum, difference, product, or quotient.

1. 43 72 69 57 + 32	**2.** 398,205 + 674,378	**3.** 483 964 827 + 691
4. 705,312 − 95,605	**5.** 869,403 − 351,674	**6.** 800,261 − 358,273
7. 58 × 67	**8.** 431 × 296	**9.** 308 × 207
10. 37)26,085	**11.** 402)127,434	**12.** 85)340,510

Word Problems

Solve each problem.

1. Jerry has a newsstand on a downtown corner. During one week his daily sales were 743, 956, 821, 543, 686, 915, and 842 papers. How many papers did he sell during the week?

2. Ann belongs to a bowling league. Her scores on six lines of bowling were 183, 252, 196, 142, 221, and 125. What was her total for the six lines?

3. Margarita is reading a book that has 1,247 pages in it. She has read 869 pages. How many pages are left?

4. The school band is collecting coupons that will save money on new uniforms. They have collected 8,952 coupons and need a total of 15,000. How many are yet to be collected?

5. The city library subscribes to 125 magazines at an average cost of $23 a year for each. What is the yearly cost of all of these magazines?

6. Bill averages 14 km per liter of gasoline on his new compact car. How many liters of gasoline will he need to drive 112 km?

7. A profit of $281,295 is to be divided equally among 47 stockholders. How much is each share?

8. Daiji spends a total of $300 for lunches over a period of 75 days. What is the average amount he spends each day?

Basic Computation Series 2000: Quizzes and Tests

Word Problems

Solve each problem.

1. Paul's scores for five pinball machine games were 87,550; 52,120; 69,000; 142,640; and 121,100. What was the total of his five scores?	**2.** Sonia spent $53, $120, $184, $215 and $76 for clothes during the school year. What was her total expenditure for clothes for the year?
3. During a bicycle race, Carol rode 21,550 meters and Gina rode 27,445 meters. How much farther did Gina ride than Carol?	**4.** Barbara had $2,641 in her checking account and decided to put $840 of it into her savings account. How much was left in the checking account after the transfer?
5. One hundred fifty people attended an awards banquet. Each paid $12 for a ticket. What the total value of the 150 tickets?	**6.** A train travels an average of 72 km per hour over a certain track. How many kilometers will it travel in 62 hours?
7. A hiker walked 560 km in 35 days. How many kilometers did he average each day?	**8.** A truck was loaded with sacks of potatoes. The total mass of the 550 sacks in the load was 24,750 kilograms. If each sack had the same mass, how many kilograms of potatoes were in each sack?

Word Problems

Solve each problem.

---

1. Ms. Bailey took a week to drive from San Francisco to New York City. The daily distances travelled were 312, 348, 365, 300, 381, 320, and 337 miles. What the total number of miles she drove on the trip?

2. Joey earned the following amounts during the twelve months of last year: $158, $160, $182, $112, $125, $110, $205, $210, $120, $133, $150, and $203. What were his total earnings for the year?

---

3. The total surface area of the state of Oklahoma is 69,919 square miles. If 1,137 square miles of this surface area is water, how many square miles is land?

4. The Peachtree Center Plaza Hotel in Atlanta, Georgia is 723 feet high. The World Trade Center in New York City is 1,368 feet high. How many feet higher is the World Trade Center than the Peachtree Center Plaza Hotel?

---

5. Willie collected $27 from each of 15 players on the football team to pay for a skiing trip they planned. What was the total amount of money he collected?

6. A bookstore has 253 shelves, each holding 155 books. If the shelves are full, how many books are there?

---

7. Shurvonne drove her car 1,938 miles on 51 gallons of gasoline. How many miles per gallon did she average?

8. Warren paid a total of $9,792 for house payments in 12 equal monthly payments. How much was each payment?

Word Problems

Solve each problem.

1. On six tests during a semester, a mathematics student earned the following points: 92, 86, 143, 135, 63, and 98. What was the total number of points earned on the six tests?	**2.** Alaska has a total surface area of 586,412 square miles, Texas has 267,338 square miles, California has 158,693 square miles, Montana has 147,138 square miles, and New Mexico has 121,666 square miles. What is the total surface area of these five states?
3. Gannett Peak, at 13,804 feet, is the highest point in the state of Wyoming. The Belle Fourche River, at 3,099 feet, is the lowest point in the state. What is the difference in these two altitudes?	**4.** Dale borrowed $85,500 and paid back $17,625. How much does he still owe on the loan?
5. DeVaun rode 32 miles on the commuter train for each of 240 days. What was the total number of miles he rode the train for these days?	**6.** A certain auto manufacturing plant produces 57 cars per day for each of the 365 days in the year. What is the total yearly auto production in this plant?
7. There are 265 textbooks for a science class. They cost a total of $5,830. Each book costs the same amount. What is the cost of each book?	**8.** A motorcycle costs $2,548. Lynne earns $26 each day. How many days must she work in order to pay for the motorcycle?

Proportions

Replace the ? with = or ≠ to make a true statement.

1. $\frac{3}{4}$? $\frac{30}{40}$	**2.** $\frac{35}{56}$? $\frac{15}{21}$	**3.** $\frac{38}{40}$? $\frac{21}{27}$

Complete each of the following by replacing the ? in each statement to make a proportion.

4. $\frac{16}{30} = \frac{?}{150}$	**5.** $\frac{?}{14} = \frac{13}{182}$	**6.** $\frac{36}{?} = \frac{12}{7}$
7. $\frac{11}{24} = \frac{?}{96}$	**8.** $\frac{?}{90} = \frac{13}{15}$	**9.** $\frac{6}{19} = \frac{48}{?}$
10. $\frac{56}{?} = \frac{7}{23}$	**11.** $\frac{5}{7} = \frac{?}{49}$	**12.** $\frac{10}{19} = \frac{90}{?}$

Proportions

Replace the ? with = or ≠ to make a true statement.

1. $\frac{6}{9}$? $\frac{14}{20}$	**2.** $\frac{28}{32}$? $\frac{70}{75}$	**3.** $\frac{18}{21}$? $\frac{72}{84}$

Complete each of the following by replacing the ? in each statement to make a proportion.

4. $\frac{36}{60} = \frac{12}{?}$	**5.** $\frac{?}{5} = \frac{16}{20}$	**6.** $\frac{49}{42} = \frac{?}{6}$
7. $\frac{88}{99} = \frac{8}{?}$	**8.** $\frac{5}{?} = \frac{35}{49}$	**9.** $\frac{27}{36} = \frac{?}{4}$
10. $\frac{60}{66} = \frac{10}{?}$	**11.** $\frac{?}{7} = \frac{40}{56}$	**12.** $\frac{7}{?} = \frac{91}{156}$

Proportions

Replace the ? with = or ≠ to make a true statement.

1. $\frac{10}{12}$? $\frac{35}{30}$	**2.** $\frac{27}{33}$? $\frac{72}{88}$	**3.** $\frac{45}{54}$? $\frac{30}{36}$

Complete each of the following by replacing the ? in each statement to make a proportion.

4. $\frac{84}{91} = \frac{?}{13}$	**5.** $\frac{12}{36} = \frac{?}{72}$	**6.** $\frac{4}{25} = \frac{16}{?}$
7. $\frac{?}{88} = \frac{3}{8}$	**8.** $\frac{9}{?} = \frac{81}{108}$	**9.** $\frac{?}{9} = \frac{24}{54}$
10. $\frac{14}{12} = \frac{7}{?}$	**11.** $\frac{?}{5} = \frac{45}{25}$	**12.** $\frac{55}{30} = \frac{11}{?}$

Proportions

Replace the ? with = or ≠ to make a true statement.

1. $\frac{42}{54}$? $\frac{56}{70}$	**2.** $\frac{30}{34}$? $\frac{60}{88}$	**3.** $\frac{56}{76}$? $\frac{42}{57}$

Complete each of the following by replacing the ? in each statement to make a proportion.

4. $\frac{48}{75} = \frac{?}{125}$	**5.** $\frac{?}{8} = \frac{63}{72}$	**6.** $\frac{192}{84} = \frac{?}{7}$
7. $\frac{1}{?} = \frac{16}{64}$	**8.** $\frac{55}{121} = \frac{5}{?}$	**9.** $\frac{?}{13} = \frac{56}{91}$
10. $\frac{72}{117} = \frac{?}{13}$	**11.** $\frac{48}{112} = \frac{3}{?}$	**12.** $\frac{5}{?} = \frac{160}{256}$

Addition of Fractions

Find each sum. Write answers in simplest form.

1. $\dfrac{2}{3}$ $+\dfrac{5}{6}$	**2.** $\dfrac{3}{4}$ $+\dfrac{3}{8}$	**3.** $\dfrac{4}{5}$ $+\dfrac{7}{10}$
4. $\dfrac{2}{7}$ $+\dfrac{5}{14}$	**5.** $\dfrac{1}{3}$ $+\dfrac{3}{4}$	**6.** $\dfrac{1}{4}$ $+\dfrac{4}{5}$
7. $\dfrac{2}{5}$ $+\dfrac{1}{6}$	**8.** $\dfrac{2}{3}$ $+\dfrac{3}{8}$	**9.** $\dfrac{5}{6}$ $+\dfrac{4}{9}$
10. $\dfrac{3}{4}$ $+\dfrac{5}{6}$	**11.** $\dfrac{5}{6}$ $+\dfrac{3}{10}$	**12.** $\dfrac{3}{10}$ $+\dfrac{7}{15}$

Addition of Fractions

Find each sum. Write answers in simplest form.

1. $\dfrac{2}{7}$ $+\dfrac{5}{14}$	**2.** $\dfrac{1}{5}$ $+\dfrac{9}{10}$	**3.** $\dfrac{1}{4}$ $+\dfrac{7}{8}$
4. $\dfrac{1}{6}$ $+\dfrac{2}{3}$	**5.** $\dfrac{1}{3}$ $+\dfrac{4}{7}$	**6.** $\dfrac{4}{7}$ $+\dfrac{2}{7}$
7. $\dfrac{3}{5}$ $+\dfrac{5}{6}$	**8.** $\dfrac{1}{4}$ $+\dfrac{3}{5}$	**9.** $\dfrac{2}{3}$ $+\dfrac{1}{4}$
10. $\dfrac{1}{4}$ $+\dfrac{7}{10}$	**11.** $\dfrac{1}{3}$ $+\dfrac{11}{15}$	**12.** $\dfrac{3}{10}$ $+\dfrac{8}{15}$

Addition of Fractions

Find each sum. Write answers in simplest form.

1. $\quad \dfrac{1}{4}$

$\quad + \dfrac{2}{3}$

2. $\quad \dfrac{3}{4}$

$\quad + \dfrac{1}{5}$

3. $\quad \dfrac{2}{5}$

$\quad + \dfrac{5}{6}$

4. $\quad \dfrac{2}{5}$

$\quad + \dfrac{3}{7}$

5. $\quad \dfrac{1}{3}$

$\quad + \dfrac{2}{7}$

6. $\quad \dfrac{5}{7}$

$\quad + \dfrac{3}{14}$

7. $\quad \dfrac{2}{5}$

$\quad + \dfrac{9}{10}$

8. $\quad \dfrac{3}{4}$

$\quad + \dfrac{1}{8}$

9. $\quad \dfrac{1}{3}$

$\quad + \dfrac{5}{6}$

10. $\quad \dfrac{3}{4}$

$\quad + \dfrac{7}{10}$

11. $\quad \dfrac{1}{6}$

$\quad + \dfrac{13}{15}$

12. $\quad \dfrac{9}{10}$

$\quad + \dfrac{11}{15}$

Addition of Fractions

Find each sum. Write answers in simplest form.

1. $\dfrac{2}{3}$ $+\dfrac{4}{7}$	**2.** $\dfrac{3}{5}$ $+\dfrac{4}{7}$	**3.** $\dfrac{4}{5}$ $+\dfrac{1}{6}$
4. $\dfrac{3}{4}$ $+\dfrac{1}{5}$	**5.** $\dfrac{1}{3}$ $+\dfrac{1}{4}$	**6.** $\dfrac{1}{3}$ $+\dfrac{5}{6}$
7. $\dfrac{3}{4}$ $+\dfrac{7}{8}$	**8.** $\dfrac{2}{5}$ $+\dfrac{3}{10}$	**9.** $\dfrac{5}{7}$ $+\dfrac{3}{14}$
10. $\dfrac{1}{4}$ $+\dfrac{7}{10}$	**11.** $\dfrac{1}{10}$ $+\dfrac{4}{15}$	**12.** $\dfrac{5}{6}$ $+\dfrac{3}{10}$

Subtraction of Fractions

Find each difference. Write answers in simplest form.

1. $\dfrac{7}{8}$ $-\dfrac{1}{4}$	**2.** $\dfrac{2}{3}$ $-\dfrac{1}{2}$	**3.** $\dfrac{4}{5}$ $-\dfrac{2}{3}$
4. $\dfrac{5}{6}$ $-\dfrac{1}{8}$	**5.** $\dfrac{5}{8}$ $-\dfrac{5}{12}$	**6.** $\dfrac{4}{5}$ $-\dfrac{2}{3}$
7. $\dfrac{2}{3}$ $-\dfrac{3}{16}$	**8.** $\dfrac{4}{5}$ $-\dfrac{7}{12}$	**9.** $\dfrac{2}{3}$ $-\dfrac{3}{7}$
10. $\dfrac{5}{6}$ $-\dfrac{3}{8}$	**11.** $\dfrac{3}{4}$ $-\dfrac{2}{3}$	**12.** $\dfrac{5}{8}$ $-\dfrac{31}{64}$

Subtraction of Fractions

Find each difference. Write answers in simplest form.

1. $\dfrac{4}{9}$ $-\dfrac{1}{3}$	**2.** $\dfrac{29}{45}$ $-\dfrac{7}{15}$	**3.** $\dfrac{26}{27}$ $-\dfrac{7}{9}$
4. $\dfrac{19}{20}$ $-\dfrac{4}{5}$	**5.** $\dfrac{5}{6}$ $-\dfrac{3}{8}$	**6.** $\dfrac{3}{4}$ $-\dfrac{1}{8}$
7. $\dfrac{2}{3}$ $-\dfrac{1}{6}$	**8.** $\dfrac{2}{3}$ $-\dfrac{1}{9}$	**9.** $\dfrac{5}{6}$ $-\dfrac{5}{9}$
10. $\dfrac{5}{6}$ $-\dfrac{1}{10}$	**11.** $\dfrac{7}{8}$ $-\dfrac{5}{12}$	**12.** $\dfrac{5}{7}$ $-\dfrac{1}{4}$

Subtraction of Fractions

Find each difference. Write answers in simplest form.

1. $\dfrac{5}{8}$ $-\dfrac{1}{4}$	**2.** $\dfrac{3}{4}$ $-\dfrac{1}{3}$	**3.** $\dfrac{5}{8}$ $-\dfrac{3}{5}$
4. $\dfrac{5}{6}$ $-\dfrac{3}{7}$	**5.** $\dfrac{7}{8}$ $-\dfrac{7}{12}$	**6.** $\dfrac{4}{5}$ $-\dfrac{1}{4}$
7. $\dfrac{2}{3}$ $-\dfrac{5}{16}$	**8.** $\dfrac{4}{5}$ $-\dfrac{5}{12}$	**9.** $\dfrac{2}{3}$ $-\dfrac{3}{7}$
10. $\dfrac{5}{6}$ $-\dfrac{5}{8}$	**11.** $\dfrac{5}{7}$ $-\dfrac{2}{5}$	**12.** $\dfrac{7}{12}$ $-\dfrac{1}{4}$

Subtraction of Fractions

Find each difference. Write answers in simplest form.

1. $\dfrac{17}{64}$ $-\dfrac{1}{8}$	**2.** $\dfrac{7}{8}$ $-\dfrac{1}{6}$	**3.** $\dfrac{11}{12}$ $-\dfrac{1}{8}$
4. $\dfrac{13}{14}$ $-\dfrac{1}{10}$	**5.** $\dfrac{15}{16}$ $-\dfrac{1}{6}$	**6.** $\dfrac{7}{12}$ $-\dfrac{1}{4}$
7. $\dfrac{6}{7}$ $-\dfrac{2}{21}$	**8.** $\dfrac{5}{6}$ $-\dfrac{1}{5}$	**9.** $\dfrac{1}{4}$ $-\dfrac{1}{14}$
10. $\dfrac{4}{15}$ $-\dfrac{1}{9}$	**11.** $\dfrac{73}{75}$ $-\dfrac{4}{15}$	**12.** $\dfrac{3}{10}$ $-\dfrac{2}{15}$

NAME _____ DATE _____

Multiplication of Fractions

Find each product. Write answers in simplest form.

1. $\frac{2}{15} \times \frac{11}{10} = ?$	**2.** $\frac{5}{8} \times \frac{48}{55} = ?$	**3.** Multiply $\frac{6}{13}$ by $\frac{52}{96}$.
4. Multiply $\frac{55}{70}$ by $\frac{7}{11}$.	**5.** $\frac{200}{500} \times \frac{45}{62} = ?$	**6.** $\frac{2}{5} \times \frac{3}{7} = ?$
7. Find the product of $\frac{33}{170}$ and $\frac{173}{55}$.	**8.** $\frac{5}{27} \times \frac{10}{27} = ?$	**9.** Multiply $\frac{7}{8}$, $\frac{2}{21}$, and $\frac{6}{15}$.
10. $11 \times \frac{7}{9} = ?$	**11.** Find the product of 13 and $\frac{5}{338}$.	**12.** $\frac{9}{35} \times \frac{5}{6} \times \frac{42}{99} = ?$

Multiplication of Fractions

Find each product. Write answers in simplest form.

1. $\frac{3}{16} \times \frac{1}{15} = ?$	**2.** $\frac{8}{35} \times \frac{5}{72} = ?$	**3.** Multiply $\frac{5}{16}$ by $\frac{64}{125}$.
4. Multiply $\frac{77}{90}$ by $\frac{10}{7}$.	**5.** $\frac{2}{3} \times \frac{5}{7} = ?$	**6.** Find the product of $\frac{55}{203}$ and $\frac{203}{66}$.
7. $\frac{3}{23} \times \frac{2}{23} = ?$	**8.** $6 \times \frac{36}{45} = ?$	**9.** Multiply $\frac{2}{3}, \frac{3}{5},$ and $\frac{5}{18}$.
10. $18 \times \frac{5}{8} = ?$	**11.** Find the product of 7 and $\frac{11}{462}$.	**12.** $\frac{5}{7} \times \frac{56}{90} \times \frac{6}{40} = ?$

Multiplication of Fractions

Find each product. Write answers in simplest form.

1. Find the product of $\frac{44}{56}$ and $\frac{28}{55}$.	**2.** $\frac{108}{132} \times \frac{11}{12} = ?$	**3.** Multiply $\frac{14}{26}$ by $\frac{13}{42}$.
4. $\frac{13}{49} \times \frac{7}{39} = ?$	**5.** $\frac{14}{26} \times \frac{13}{15} \times \frac{49}{56} = ?$	**6.** Find the product of $\frac{106}{136}$ and $\frac{15}{20}$.
7. $\frac{5}{11} \times \frac{6}{31} = ?$	**8.** $15 \times \frac{13}{45} = ?$	**9.** Multiply $\frac{58}{64}$ by $\frac{8}{29}$.
10. $20 \times \frac{2}{5} = ?$	**11.** Find the product of $\frac{18}{21}$ and $\frac{21}{9}$.	**12.** $\frac{18}{20} \times \frac{56}{20} \times \frac{8}{9} = ?$

Multiplication of Fractions

Find each product. Write answers in simplest form.

1. $\dfrac{3}{14} \times \dfrac{5}{6} \times \dfrac{7}{15} = ?$	**2.** $\dfrac{3}{4} \times \dfrac{11}{39} \times \dfrac{8}{77} = ?$	**3.** $\dfrac{16}{25} \times \dfrac{3}{8} \times \dfrac{9}{28} = ?$
4. $\dfrac{15}{32} \times \dfrac{8}{25} \times \dfrac{5}{22} = ?$	**5.** $\dfrac{6}{13} \times \dfrac{26}{39} \times \dfrac{15}{42} = ?$	**6.** $\dfrac{16}{35} \times \dfrac{14}{45} \times \dfrac{25}{36} = ?$
7. $\dfrac{34}{57} \times \dfrac{49}{51} \times \dfrac{38}{63} = ?$	**8.** $\dfrac{32}{75} \times \dfrac{45}{10} \times \dfrac{50}{27} = ?$	**9.** $\dfrac{12}{35} \times \dfrac{13}{27} \times \dfrac{14}{39} = ?$
10. $\dfrac{2}{3} \times 15 = ?$	**11.** $44 \times \dfrac{13}{11} = ?$	**12.** Multiply $\dfrac{18}{53}$ by $\dfrac{106}{16}$.

Division of Fractions

Find each quotient. Write answers in simplest form.

1. $\dfrac{12}{15} \div \dfrac{9}{45} = ?$	**2.** $\dfrac{\frac{22}{32}}{\frac{6}{8}} = ?$	**3.** Divide 9 by $\dfrac{3}{5}$.
4. Divide $\dfrac{8}{21}$ by 8.	**5.** $\dfrac{36}{48} \div \dfrac{3}{4} = ?$	**6.** $\dfrac{\frac{7}{25}}{\frac{21}{50}} = ?$
7. $\dfrac{3}{7} \div \dfrac{2}{5} = ?$	**8.** Divide $\dfrac{49}{60}$ by $\dfrac{7}{15}$.	**9.** $\dfrac{45}{52} \div 30 = ?$
10. Divide $\dfrac{51}{3}$ by 17.	**11.** $\dfrac{32}{75} \div \dfrac{8}{150} = ?$	**12.** $28 \div \dfrac{7}{8} = ?$

Division of Fractions

Find each quotient. Write answers in simplest form.

1. $\frac{3}{8} \div \frac{1}{2} = ?$	**2.** Divide $\frac{3}{50}$ by $\frac{7}{10}$.	**3.** $\dfrac{\frac{5}{6}}{\frac{5}{42}} = ?$
4. Divide $\frac{9}{24}$ by $\frac{3}{8}$.	**5.** $\dfrac{\frac{25}{39}}{\frac{15}{13}} = ?$	**6.** $\frac{20}{700} \div \frac{5}{7} = ?$
7. $\dfrac{\frac{5}{6}}{\frac{25}{34}} = ?$	**8.** Divide $\frac{1}{4}$ by 7.	**9.** $\frac{16}{173} \div \frac{20}{173} = ?$
10. Divide $\frac{7}{8}$ by 2.	**11.** $\frac{1}{7} \div \frac{1}{2} = ?$	**12.** $\dfrac{\frac{30}{41}}{\frac{5}{6}} = ?$

Division of Fractions

Find each quotient. Write answers in simplest form.

1. $\frac{5}{9} \div \frac{1}{3} = ?$	**2.** Divide $\frac{11}{30}$ by $\frac{33}{20}$.	**3.** $\dfrac{\frac{7}{8}}{\frac{7}{4}} = ?$
4. Divide $\frac{16}{63}$ by $\frac{44}{56}$.	**5.** $\dfrac{\frac{15}{36}}{\frac{55}{42}} = ?$	**6.** $\frac{40}{300} \div \frac{48}{27} = ?$
7. $\dfrac{\frac{8}{9}}{\frac{18}{15}} = ?$	**8.** Divide $\frac{1}{3}$ by 8.	**9.** $\frac{18}{199} \div \frac{15}{199} = ?$
10. Divide $\frac{9}{8}$ by 3.	**11.** $\frac{1}{2} \div \frac{1}{7} = ?$	**12.** $\dfrac{\frac{28}{51}}{\frac{7}{3}} = ?$

Division of Fractions

Find each quotient. Write answers in simplest form.

1. $\dfrac{3}{5} \div \dfrac{9}{10} = ?$	**2.** $\dfrac{5}{6} \div \dfrac{7}{12} = ?$	**3.** $\dfrac{\frac{3}{4}}{6} = ?$
4. Divide $\dfrac{3}{4}$ by $\dfrac{3}{8}$.	**5.** $5 \div \dfrac{15}{16} = ?$	**6.** $\dfrac{\frac{2}{3}}{\frac{5}{8}} = ?$
7. $\dfrac{\frac{7}{8}}{\frac{5}{6}} = ?$	**8.** Divide 4 by $\dfrac{2}{5}$.	**9.** $\dfrac{9}{16} \div \dfrac{2}{5} = ?$
10. Divide $\dfrac{1}{4}$ by $\dfrac{3}{4}$.	**11.** $\dfrac{7}{\frac{1}{8}} = ?$	**12.** $6 \div \dfrac{4}{5} = ?$

Basic Computation Series 2000: Quizzes and Tests

Operations with Fractions

Find each sum, difference, product, or quotient. Write answers in simplest form.

1. $\dfrac{5}{13}$ $+\dfrac{7}{39}$	**2.** $\dfrac{1}{2}$ $\dfrac{2}{3}$ $+\dfrac{13}{14}$	**3.** $\dfrac{3}{16}$ $+\dfrac{17}{20}$
4. $\dfrac{3}{4}$ $-\dfrac{5}{12}$	**5.** Find the difference between $\dfrac{5}{8}$ and $\dfrac{1}{4}$.	**6.** Subtract $\dfrac{7}{10}$ from $\dfrac{13}{16}$.
7. $\dfrac{3}{14} \times \dfrac{5}{6} \times \dfrac{7}{15} = ?$	**8.** Find the product of $\dfrac{3}{4}$, $\dfrac{11}{39}$, and $\dfrac{8}{77}$.	**9.** $\dfrac{16}{15} \times \dfrac{3}{8} \times \dfrac{9}{28} = ?$
10. $\dfrac{3}{7} \div \dfrac{15}{14} = ?$	**11.** Divide $\dfrac{64}{60}$ by $\dfrac{6}{8}$.	**12.** $\dfrac{\frac{8}{21}}{\frac{3}{10}} = ?$

Operations with Fractions

Find each sum, difference, product, or quotient. Write answers in simplest form.

1. Find the sum of $\frac{5}{17}$ and $\frac{45}{51}$.	**2.** $\begin{array}{r} \frac{2}{15} \\ \frac{3}{4} \\ + \frac{7}{12} \\ \hline \end{array}$	**3.** $\frac{3}{16} + \frac{17}{20} = ?$
4. $\frac{4}{5} - \frac{3}{4} = ?$	**5.** Find the difference between $\frac{5}{6}$ and $\frac{3}{8}$.	**6.** Subtract $\frac{21}{32}$ from $\frac{15}{16}$.
7. $\frac{15}{32} \times \frac{8}{25} \times \frac{5}{22} = ?$	**8.** Find the product of $\frac{6}{13}$, $\frac{26}{45}$, and $\frac{15}{42}$.	**9.** $\frac{16}{35} \times \frac{14}{45} \times \frac{25}{36} = ?$
10. $\frac{13}{48} \div \frac{39}{136} = ?$	**11.** Divide $\frac{32}{45}$ by $\frac{8}{5}$.	**12.** $\dfrac{\frac{10}{51}}{\frac{25}{34}} = ?$

Basic Computation Series 2000: Quizzes and Tests

NAME_____ DATE_____

Operations with Fractions

Find each sum, difference, product, or quotient. Write answers in simplest form.

1. $\frac{3}{5} + \frac{7}{19} = ?$	**2.** $\begin{array}{r} \frac{5}{6} \\ \frac{3}{8} \\ +\frac{7}{16} \\ \hline \end{array}$	**3.** Add $\frac{7}{16}$ and $\frac{41}{48}$.
4. $\frac{11}{16} - \frac{9}{20} = ?$	**5.** Find the difference between $\frac{7}{8}$ and $\frac{2}{3}$.	**6.** Subtract $\frac{7}{16}$ from $\frac{2}{3}$.
7. $\frac{34}{57} \times \frac{49}{51} \times \frac{38}{63} = ?$	**8.** Find the product of $\frac{12}{35}$, $\frac{13}{27}$, and $\frac{14}{39}$.	**9.** $\frac{32}{75} \times \frac{45}{10} \times \frac{50}{27} = ?$
10. $\frac{100}{200} \div \frac{7}{8} = ?$	**11.** Divide 8 by $\frac{7}{10}$.	**12.** $\frac{\frac{7}{8}}{\frac{3}{4}} = ?$

Basic Computation Series 2000: Quizzes and Tests   **67**

Operations with Fractions

Find each sum, difference, product, or quotient. Write answers in simplest form.

1. Find the sum of $\frac{20}{63}$ and $\frac{4}{7}$.	**2.** $\quad\frac{2}{3}$ $\quad\frac{4}{17}$ $+\frac{26}{51}$ ————	**3.** Add $\frac{11}{20}$ and $\frac{3}{35}$.
4. $\quad\frac{3}{5}$ $-\frac{7}{12}$ ————	**5.** Find the difference between $\frac{5}{16}$ and $\frac{7}{8}$.	**6.** Subtract $\frac{3}{4}$ from $\frac{11}{12}$.
7. $\frac{6}{35} \times \frac{5}{16} \times \frac{28}{27} = ?$	**8.** Find the product of $\frac{14}{39}$, $\frac{13}{66}$, and $\frac{55}{56}$.	**9.** $\frac{9}{63} \times \frac{15}{45} \times \frac{42}{99} = ?$
10. $\frac{1}{8} \div \frac{1}{6} = ?$	**11.** Divide $\frac{36}{55}$ by 4.	**12.** $\dfrac{\frac{65}{72}}{\frac{5}{12}} = ?$

Addition of Mixed Numbers

Find each sum. Write answers in simplest form.

1. $4\frac{3}{5}$ $+\,9\frac{1}{6}$	**2.** Find the sum of $2\frac{3}{4}$ and $2\frac{1}{12}$.	**3.** $2\frac{9}{16}$ $+\,\frac{23}{32}$
4. $7\frac{11}{12}$ $2\frac{3}{10}$ $+\,6\,\frac{3}{5}$	**5.** $7\frac{5}{6}$ $+\,1\frac{3}{4}$	**6.** $9\frac{5}{9}$ $+\,4\frac{8}{9}$
7. $5\frac{13}{16}$ $+\,6\,\frac{1}{2}$	**8.** $5\frac{9}{10}$ $+\,1\frac{2}{5}$	**9.** $9\frac{2}{3} + 5\frac{5}{6} + 1\frac{1}{4} = ?$
10. $5\,\frac{2}{3}$ $+\,2\frac{9}{10}$	**11.** $7\,\frac{1}{2}$ $2\frac{3}{10}$ $+\,6\,\frac{3}{5}$	**12.** $4\,\frac{3}{7}$ $+\,3\frac{11}{14}$

Addition of Mixed Numbers

Find each sum. Write answers in simplest form.

1. $2\frac{1}{4}$ $+\ 3\frac{3}{8}$	**2.** $9\frac{11}{12} + 10\frac{4}{9} = ?$	**3.** Find the sum of $6\frac{3}{4}$, $2\frac{1}{8}$, and $9\frac{1}{2}$.
4. Add $8\frac{3}{4}$ and $9\frac{2}{7}$.	**5.** $8\ \frac{4}{9}$ $+\ 2\frac{5}{12}$	**6.** $7\frac{1}{5}$ $+\ 5\frac{3}{4}$
7. $9\frac{13}{16}$ $+\ 1\ \frac{1}{5}$	**8.** $10\ \frac{1}{17}$ $+\ 9\ \frac{2}{51}$	**9.** 8 $2\frac{1}{3}$ $+\ 5\frac{3}{4}$
10. $6\frac{1}{2}$ $+\ 8\frac{2}{5}$	**11.** $3\ \frac{1}{5}$ $\frac{2}{3}$ $+\ 6\frac{4}{15}$	**12.** $9\ \frac{3}{5}$ $+\ 3\frac{1}{10}$

Addition of Mixed Numbers

Find each sum. Write answers in simplest form.

1. $4\frac{3}{10}$ $+\ \ \frac{7}{8}$	**2.** $2\frac{1}{2}$ $3\frac{4}{5}$ $+\ 1\frac{2}{3}$	**3.** $2\frac{1}{3}$ $4\frac{1}{6}$ $+\ 5\frac{1}{8}$
4. $5\frac{13}{16}$ $+\ 6\frac{1}{2}$	**5.** $11\frac{5}{6}$ $+\ \ 3\frac{7}{10}$	**6.** $1\frac{5}{6}$ $+\ 8\frac{11}{12}$
7. Add $10\frac{7}{12}$ and $18\frac{15}{16}$.	**8.** $3\frac{19}{32} + 1\frac{11}{16} + 5\frac{3}{4} = ?$	**9.** $13\frac{5}{12}$ $+\ \ \ \frac{11}{12}$
10. $4\frac{3}{5}$ $+\ 9\frac{1}{6}$	**11.** $23\frac{7}{10}$ $+\ 18\frac{2}{3}$	**12.** $6\frac{7}{12}$ $+\ 7\frac{7}{9}$

Addition of Mixed Numbers

Find each sum. Write answers in simplest form.

1. $12\frac{7}{8}$ $+\ 3\frac{5}{8}$	**2.** $6\frac{3}{8}$ $+\ 2\frac{1}{4}$	**3.** Find the sum of $8\frac{1}{12}$ and $7\frac{9}{16}$.
4. Add $4\frac{1}{5}$ and $2\frac{7}{15}$.	**5.** $3\frac{2}{15}$ $+\ \ \frac{2}{3}$	**6.** $3\frac{7}{9}+2\frac{1}{3}+3\frac{5}{6}=\ ?$
7. $21\frac{5}{6}$ $+\ 3\frac{11}{12}$	**8.** $15\frac{17}{20}$ $+\ 12\frac{7}{8}$	**9.** $4\frac{7}{25}+2\frac{3}{4}=\ ?$
10. Find the sum of $11\frac{17}{20}$ and $4\frac{3}{4}$.	**11.** $3\frac{3}{8}$ $+\ 1\frac{5}{16}$	**12.** $7\frac{2}{3}$ $+\ 4\frac{3}{5}$

Subtraction of Mixed Numbers

Find each difference. Write answers in simplest form.

1. $9\frac{5}{8}$
  $-\,4\frac{1}{4}$
	2. $35\frac{1}{4}$
	  $-\,15$
		3. $40\frac{3}{4}-39\frac{1}{4}=\,?$

4. $3\frac{1}{2}$
  $-\,1\frac{1}{4}$
	5. $17\frac{13}{16}$
	  $-\,9\frac{5}{8}$
		6. $12\frac{5}{8}$
		  $-\,9\frac{1}{16}$

7. Subtract $2\frac{1}{3}$ from $3\frac{3}{4}$.	**8.** $5\frac{5}{16}$ $-\,2\frac{15}{16}$	**9.** $2\frac{3}{8}-\frac{5}{16}=\,?$
10. Find the difference between $62\frac{1}{3}$ and $27\frac{1}{3}$.	**11.** $11\frac{7}{8}$ $-\,3\frac{3}{10}$	**12.** How much greater than $4\frac{1}{3}$ is $7\frac{1}{2}$?

Subtraction of Mixed Numbers

Find each difference. Write answers in simplest form.

1. $9\frac{3}{16}$ $-\ 2\frac{5}{6}$	**2.** $11\frac{5}{8}$ $-\ 4$	**3.** 9 $-\ 2\frac{11}{16}$
4. $8\frac{1}{2} - 4\frac{2}{3} = ?$	**5.** 6 $-\ \frac{7}{8}$	**6.** Subtract $1\frac{15}{16}$ from $4\frac{1}{4}$.
7. How much greater than $2\frac{1}{3}$ is $3\frac{3}{5}$?	**8.** $9\frac{3}{8}$ $-\ 3\frac{15}{32}$	**9.** $5\frac{7}{8} - 3\frac{1}{2} = ?$
10. $5\frac{2}{3}$ $-\ 2\frac{9}{10}$	**11.** $7\frac{2}{3}$ $-\ 4\frac{1}{4}$	**12.** $18\frac{7}{12}$ $-\ 10\frac{5}{12}$

Subtraction of Mixed Numbers

Find each difference. Write answers in simplest form.

1. $3\frac{1}{2}$ $-\ 3\frac{1}{4}$	**2.** $11\frac{3}{5}$ $-\ 9\frac{1}{4}$	**3.** $22\frac{5}{8}$ $-\ 12\frac{1}{2}$
4. Subtract $4\frac{3}{4}$ from $12\frac{5}{8}$.	**5.** $25\frac{7}{9}$ $-\ 16\frac{7}{12}$	**6.** $17\frac{2}{3}$ $-\ 15\frac{3}{4}$
7. How much greater than $4\frac{3}{4}$ is $5\frac{1}{8}$?	**8.** $10\frac{9}{10}$ $-\ 7\frac{1}{4}$	**9.** $13\frac{3}{4}$ $-\ 11\frac{3}{7}$
10. $10\frac{1}{3} - 8\frac{3}{4} = ?$	**11.** $9\frac{1}{2}$ $-\ 6\frac{3}{4}$	**12.** $34\frac{3}{5}$ $-\ 29\frac{1}{2}$

Subtraction of Mixed Numbers

Find each difference. Write answers in simplest form.

1. $32\frac{4}{5}$ $-19\frac{2}{3}$	**2.** Find the difference between $62\frac{1}{6}$ and $27\frac{1}{3}$.	**3.** $19\frac{5}{16}$ $-12\frac{1}{4}$
4. $15\frac{3}{8}$ $-14\frac{4}{5}$	**5.** $34\frac{5}{7}$ $-29\frac{1}{2}$	**6.** $15\frac{3}{16}$ $-14\frac{7}{8}$
7. $5\frac{9}{10}$ $-4\frac{5}{6}$	**8.** $12\frac{5}{8}$ $-9\frac{1}{6}$	**9.** $17\frac{3}{4}$ $-5\frac{7}{8}$
10. Subtract $1\frac{3}{4}$ from $21\frac{1}{2}$.	**11.** Find the difference between $6\frac{5}{8}$ and $4\frac{3}{4}$.	**12.** $8\frac{2}{3}-5\frac{1}{2}=?$

Multiplication of Mixed Numbers

Find each product. Write answers in simplest form.

1. $4\frac{1}{3} \times 3\frac{1}{5} = ?$	**2.** $5\frac{3}{5} \times 3\frac{4}{7} = ?$	**3.** $2\frac{1}{7} \times 2\frac{4}{5} = ?$
4. $7\frac{7}{10} \times 2\frac{1}{12} = ?$	**5.** $5\frac{7}{8} \times 1\frac{3}{47} = ?$	**6.** $3\frac{1}{8} \times 18 = ?$
7. $15 \times 2\frac{1}{5} = ?$	**8.** $3\frac{1}{7} \times 2\frac{1}{2} = ?$	**9.** $3\frac{1}{3} \times 10\frac{1}{2} = ?$
10. $11\frac{2}{3} \times 1\frac{4}{5} = ?$	**11.** $9\frac{5}{6} \times 7\frac{3}{8} = ?$	**12.** $4\frac{1}{11} \times 8\frac{5}{9} = ?$

Multiplication of Mixed Numbers

Find each product. Write answers in simplest form.

1. $3\frac{1}{5} \times 2\frac{1}{4} = ?$	**2.** $7\frac{2}{3} \times 1\frac{1}{4} = ?$	**3.** $4\frac{1}{5} \times 4\frac{2}{7} = ?$
4. $5\frac{1}{3} \times 4\frac{1}{2} = ?$	**5.** $6\frac{2}{5} \times 6\frac{3}{7} = ?$	**6.** $8\frac{1}{3} \times 9\frac{4}{5} = ?$
7. $3\frac{5}{6} \times 2\frac{5}{8} = ?$	**8.** $9\frac{7}{9} \times 3\frac{3}{4} = ?$	**9.** $7\frac{1}{4} \times 3\frac{1}{5} = ?$
10. $3\frac{1}{5} \times 2\frac{1}{2} = ?$	**11.** $3\frac{1}{2} \times 2\frac{2}{7} = ?$	**12.** $1\frac{4}{5} \times \frac{5}{18} = ?$

Multiplication of Mixed Numbers

Find each product. Write answers in simplest form.

1. $20 \times 2\frac{1}{8} = ?$	**2.** $7\frac{1}{5} \times \frac{5}{6} = ?$	**3.** $6\frac{5}{6} \times 3\frac{7}{8} = ?$
4. $5\frac{1}{7} \times 3\frac{1}{9} = ?$	**5.** $2\frac{5}{8} \times 1\frac{1}{63} = ?$	**6.** $3\frac{1}{7} \times 1\frac{10}{11} = ?$
7. $9\frac{4}{5} \times 3\frac{4}{7} = ?$	**8.** $4\frac{3}{8} \times 4\frac{4}{5} = ?$	**9.** $5\frac{3}{5} \times 10\frac{5}{7} = ?$
10. $10\frac{1}{2} \times 2\frac{1}{7} = ?$	**11.** $1\frac{7}{15} \times 6\frac{2}{3} = ?$	**12.** $4\frac{12}{13} \times 4\frac{7}{8} = ?$

Multiplication of Mixed Numbers

Find each product. Write answers in simplest form.

1. $5\frac{3}{5} \times 1\frac{13}{21} = ?$	**2.** $5\frac{1}{5} \times 12\frac{1}{2} = ?$	**3.** $2\frac{4}{5} \times 5\frac{5}{7} = ?$
4. $7\frac{1}{2} \times 2\frac{2}{5} = ?$	**5.** $1\frac{1}{9} \times 4\frac{1}{5} = ?$	**6.** $5\frac{5}{7} \times 2\frac{1}{10} = ?$
7. $1\frac{1}{63} \times 2\frac{5}{8} = ?$	**8.** $9\frac{1}{3} \times 6\frac{3}{4} = ?$	**9.** $9\frac{3}{8} \times 11\frac{1}{9} = ?$
10. $3\frac{1}{3} \times 1\frac{1}{5} = ?$	**11.** $22\frac{2}{3} \times 2\frac{1}{4} = ?$	**12.** $3\frac{3}{5} \times 7\frac{1}{2} = ?$

Basic Computation Series 2000: Quizzes and Tests

Division of Mixed Numbers

Find each quotient. Write answers in simplest form.

1. $1\frac{5}{7} \div 3\frac{1}{2} = ?$	**2.** $3\frac{1}{8} \div 1\frac{1}{4} = ?$	**3.** $4\frac{1}{3} \div 1\frac{2}{3} = ?$
4. $5\frac{3}{5} \div \frac{7}{25} = ?$	**5.** $2\frac{1}{7} \div 1\frac{11}{14} = ?$	**6.** $2\frac{1}{12} \div 4\frac{1}{2} = ?$
7. $7\frac{7}{10} \div 1\frac{1}{10} = ?$	**8.** $3\frac{1}{8} \div 2\frac{1}{2} = ?$	**9.** $2\frac{1}{5} \div 3\frac{2}{25} = ?$
10. $3\frac{1}{3} \div 1\frac{2}{3} = ?$	**11.** $\dfrac{6\frac{2}{3}}{1\frac{1}{9}} = ?$	**12.** $\dfrac{8\frac{2}{3}}{12\frac{5}{6}} = ?$

Division of Mixed Numbers

Find each quotient. Write answers in simplest form.

1. $2\frac{1}{3} \div 3\frac{1}{9} = ?$	**2.** $2\frac{4}{5} \div 4\frac{1}{5} = ?$	**3.** $3\frac{1}{3} \div 3\frac{8}{9} = ?$
4. $6\frac{5}{6} \div \frac{5}{6} = ?$	**5.** $2\frac{4}{7} \div 1\frac{2}{7} = ?$	**6.** $16\frac{2}{3} \div 4\frac{1}{6} = ?$
7. $8\frac{1}{3} \div 6 = ?$	**8.** $4\frac{1}{6} \div 1\frac{2}{3} = ?$	**9.** $21\frac{1}{3} \div 2\frac{2}{3} = ?$
10. $2\frac{1}{3} \div 3\frac{1}{8} = ?$	**11.** $\dfrac{3\frac{4}{5}}{1\frac{3}{7}} = ?$	**12.** $\dfrac{1\frac{2}{3}}{4\frac{1}{6}} = ?$

Division of Mixed Numbers

Find each quotient. Write answers in simplest form.

1. $2\frac{1}{7} \div 1\frac{11}{14} = ?$	**2.** $3\frac{1}{2} \div 2\frac{5}{8} = ?$	**3.** $1\frac{2}{3} \div 2\frac{5}{8} = ?$
4. $2\frac{1}{2} \div 1\frac{1}{4} = ?$	**5.** $3\frac{1}{9} \div 2\frac{2}{5} = ?$	**6.** $12\frac{5}{6} \div 8\frac{2}{3} = ?$
7. $1\frac{1}{9} \div 6\frac{2}{3} = ?$	**8.** $3\frac{1}{8} \div 3\frac{1}{8} = ?$	**9.** $7 \div 2\frac{1}{3} = ?$
10. $9\frac{3}{7} \div 25\frac{2}{3} = ?$	**11.** $\dfrac{2\frac{5}{8}}{1\frac{1}{2}} = ?$	**12.** $\dfrac{1\frac{7}{8}}{7\frac{1}{4}} = ?$

Division of Mixed Numbers

Find each quotient. Write answers in simplest form.

1. $1\frac{1}{4} \div 7\frac{1}{2} = ?$	**2.** $8\frac{1}{3} \div 4\frac{1}{6} = ?$	**3.** $5\frac{1}{5} \div 1\frac{3}{10} = ?$
4. $9\frac{1}{3} \div 2\frac{2}{9} = ?$	**5.** $2\frac{1}{2} \div 1\frac{1}{6} = ?$	**6.** $3\frac{1}{7} \div 2\frac{5}{14} = ?$
7. $4\frac{1}{6} \div 8\frac{1}{3} = ?$	**8.** $1\frac{3}{10} \div 5\frac{1}{5} = ?$	**9.** $4\frac{1}{6} \div 1\frac{7}{8} = ?$
10. $5\frac{1}{7} \div 1\frac{1}{21} = ?$	**11.** $\dfrac{6\frac{3}{8}}{3\frac{1}{4}} = ?$	**12.** $\dfrac{9\frac{5}{8}}{2\frac{3}{4}} = ?$

Operations with Mixed Numbers

Find each sum, difference, product, or quotient. Write answers in simplest form.

1. $\quad 2\frac{3}{4}$ $\quad +3\frac{5}{8}$	**2.** $\quad 4\frac{11}{12}$ $\quad +2\frac{5}{12}$	**3.** $8\frac{13}{16} + 2\frac{3}{4} + 5\frac{1}{2} = ?$
4. $\quad 6\frac{13}{16}$ $\quad -2\frac{5}{16}$	**5.** $\quad 7$ $\quad -1\frac{5}{6}$	**6.** How much larger than 2 is $8\frac{1}{2}$?
7. $24 \times 4\frac{5}{8} = ?$	**8.** Find the product of $3\frac{3}{4}$ and $7\frac{1}{5}$.	**9.** $2\frac{1}{2} \times 10 = ?$
10. $6\frac{2}{3} \div 5\frac{5}{6} = ?$	**11.** $45 \div 1\frac{7}{8} = ?$	**12.** $\dfrac{12\frac{1}{4}}{4} = ?$

NAME   DATE

Operations with Mixed Numbers

Find each sum, difference, product, or quotient. Write answers in simplest form.

1. $24\frac{9}{10}$ $+ 17\frac{5}{8}$	**2.** $4\frac{1}{3}$ $8\frac{3}{8}$ $+ 2\frac{3}{4}$	**3.** $2\frac{5}{6} + 3\frac{1}{10} + 4\frac{1}{2} = ?$
4. $36\frac{2}{3}$ $- 17\frac{7}{8}$	**5.** $4 - \frac{9}{16} = ?$	**6.** Find the difference between $9\frac{1}{16}$ and $2\frac{3}{5}$.
7. $2\frac{5}{8} \times 2\frac{2}{5} = ?$	**8.** Find the product of $2\frac{7}{8}$ and $1\frac{3}{4}$.	**9.** $1\frac{3}{4} \times 18 = ?$
10. $9\frac{1}{3} \div 3\frac{1}{7} = ?$	**11.** $11\frac{1}{3} \div 2\frac{5}{6} = ?$	**12.** $\dfrac{3\frac{15}{16}}{2\frac{5}{8}} = ?$

Operations with Mixed Numbers

Find each sum, difference, product, or quotient. Write answers in simplest form.

1. $32\frac{5}{9}$ $+\ 15\frac{7}{12}$	**2.** $18\frac{5}{8}$ $13\frac{11}{12}$ $+\ 42\frac{3}{16}$	**3.** $4\frac{3}{10}+8\frac{5}{12}=?$
4. $6\frac{1}{2}-\frac{2}{3}=?$	**5.** Find the difference between $18\frac{5}{6}$ and $12\frac{15}{16}$.	**6.** 42 $-\ 17\frac{7}{20}$
7. Find the product of $2\frac{2}{3}$, $1\frac{1}{8}$, and $3\frac{5}{6}$.	**8.** $1\frac{9}{16}\times2\frac{4}{5}=?$	**9.** Multiply 7 by $3\frac{1}{4}$.
10. Divide $3\frac{3}{4}$ by $4\frac{2}{5}$.	**11.** $\dfrac{68}{3\frac{2}{5}}=?$	**12.** $62\frac{1}{2}\div100=?$

Operations with Mixed Numbers

Find each sum, difference, product, or quotient. Write answers in simplest form.

1. $16\frac{1}{3}$ $+\ 3\frac{1}{9}$	**2.** $24\frac{5}{16}$ $+\ 8\frac{1}{4}$	**3.** $14\frac{5}{6}$ $2\frac{3}{4}$ $+\ 5\frac{7}{8}$
4. $28\frac{4}{15}$ $-\ 15\frac{20}{21}$	**5.** $8\frac{1}{3}-2\frac{3}{4}=?$	**6.** Find the difference between $16\frac{1}{8}$ and $7\frac{2}{3}$.
7. $3\frac{8}{9}\times1\frac{2}{7}=?$	**8.** $4\frac{1}{7}\times2\frac{1}{10}=?$	**9.** Find the product of $3\frac{1}{5}$ and $2\frac{1}{4}$.
10. $7\frac{7}{10}\div1\frac{1}{10}=?$	**11.** $\dfrac{3\frac{3}{4}}{4\frac{3}{8}}=?$	**12.** Divide $7\frac{2}{9}$ by $4\frac{7}{12}$.

Basic Computation Series 2000: Quizzes and Tests

Word Problems

Solve each problem. Write answers in simplest form.

1. Yoshi needs three pieces of wire measuring $5\frac{1}{2}$, $28\frac{1}{2}$, and $15\frac{3}{4}$ inches. What is the total number of inches of wire he needs?	**2.** Felicia hiked $20\frac{1}{2}$ miles, $24\frac{1}{4}$ miles and $28\frac{3}{4}$ miles on three days. What is the total distance she hiked?
3. John is $69\frac{1}{2}$ inches tall. Bill is $71\frac{3}{4}$ inches tall. How much taller is Bill than John?	**4.** Rita hiked $7\frac{5}{6}$ miles. Nancy hiked $5\frac{7}{8}$ miles. How much farther did Rita hike than Nancy?
5. Ramon had $2\frac{1}{2}$ pounds of grapes. He gave his sister half of them. How many pounds did he have left?	**6.** A raisin nut cake recipe calls for $1\frac{1}{3}$ cups of raisins. The recipe is to be doubled. How many cups of raisins should be used?
7. How many one-thirds are there in $7\frac{1}{3}$?	**8.** A board $27\frac{1}{2}$ feet long is to be cut into 5 pieces. How long will each piece be?

Word Problems

Solve each problem. Write answers in simplest form.

---

1. In a relay race, Ann ran $45\frac{1}{4}$ yards, Jill ran $40\frac{1}{3}$ yards, and Dinah ran $42\frac{1}{16}$ yards. What was the total number of yards the girls ran?

2. Aramy needs 3 pieces of lumber to complete a project. The pieces measure $5\frac{3}{4}$, $3\frac{1}{2}$, and $4\frac{1}{2}$ feet. What is the total number of feet needed?

---

3. Aaron bought $3\frac{1}{2}$ pounds of fruit and $4\frac{7}{8}$ pounds of vegetables. How many more pounds of vegetables than fruit did he buy?

4. Bryan bought $2\frac{1}{2}$ pounds of oatmeal cookies. His friends ate $1\frac{7}{8}$ pounds of them. How many pounds were left?

---

5. Grant lives $2\frac{1}{4}$ miles from school. His mother drove him $\frac{1}{3}$ of this distance. How far did she drive him?

6. A lake is $3\frac{9}{16}$ miles wide. How far is it to the middle of the lake from one bank?

---

7. How many one-fourths are there in $7\frac{5}{8}$?

8. A board $8\frac{2}{3}$ feet long is to be cut into 6 pieces. How long will each piece be?

Word Problems

Solve each problem. Write answers in simplest form.

1. Angie hiked $18\frac{1}{4}$, $20\frac{1}{2}$, and $22\frac{1}{8}$ miles in three days. What is the total distance she hiked?	**2.** Peter bought $5\frac{1}{2}$ pounds of cherries, $3\frac{1}{4}$ pounds of apples, and $4\frac{1}{8}$ pounds of oranges. How many pounds of fruit did he buy?
3. D'Nisha is $66\frac{3}{4}$ inches tall. Carol is $64\frac{7}{8}$ inches tall. How much taller is D'Nisha than Carol?	**4.** June jogged $2\frac{15}{16}$ miles. Tracy jogged $3\frac{1}{2}$ miles. How much farther did Tracy jog?
5. A moving van carried $3\frac{5}{7}$ tons of furniture to a new home and unloaded $\frac{1}{4}$ of it in 2 hours. How many tons of furniture was unloaded in 2 hours?	**6.** A recipe calls for $4\frac{1}{2}$ cups of flour. The recipe is to be tripled. How much flour should be used?
7. How many one-fifths are there in $6\frac{3}{10}$?	**8.** A length of string $5\frac{1}{2}$ yards long is to be cut into 3 pieces. How long will each piece be?

Word Problems

Solve each problem. Write answers in simplest form.

---

1. Vera drove $53\frac{7}{8}$ miles, $24\frac{3}{4}$ miles, and $49\frac{1}{2}$ miles in three days. How many miles did she drive?

2. Three people in an elevator weigh $235\frac{1}{2}$ pounds, $197\frac{3}{4}$ pounds, and $142\frac{3}{16}$ pounds. What is their total weight? The capacity of the elevator is 1,000 pounds. Is the elevator overloaded?

---

3. Pearl purchased $3\frac{1}{2}$ yards of poster paper. She used $2\frac{7}{8}$ yards of it. How many yards did she have left?

4. Gary bought $7\frac{1}{2}$ feet of lumber. He used $5\frac{7}{8}$ feet of it. How much lumber did he have left?

---

5. Janet lives $2\frac{5}{8}$ miles from school. After walking $\frac{1}{3}$ of this distance, she stopped to rest. How far had she walked by then?

6. A recipe for pecan pie calls for $1\frac{1}{2}$ cups of sugar. A pie $1\frac{1}{2}$ times as large is to be made. How much sugar is needed?

---

7. How many portions of $8\frac{3}{4}$ ounces each can be cut from a boneless roast weighing 28 pounds? (1 pound = 16 ounces.)

8. A piece of cloth $7\frac{3}{4}$ yards long is to be cut into 5 pieces. How long will each piece be?

Place Value and Rounding

1. Write 3,217 in words.	**2.** Write 43.821 in words.
3. Write seventy thousand, fifty-five using numerals.	**4.** Write three hundred and one hundred twenty-two thousandths using numerals.
5. What decimal is equivalent to $\frac{1}{3}$?	**6.** What decimal is equivalent to $\frac{5}{8}$?
7. Write 0.44 as a fraction in simplest form.	**8.** Write 0.865 as a fraction in simplest form.
9. Round 3,752 to the hundreds place.	**10.** Round 56.4391 to the hundredths place.
11. Round 63,247 to the thousands place.	**12.** Round 434.176 to the tenths place.

NAME

DATE

Place Value and Rounding

1. Write 4,379 in words.	**2.** Write 476.083 in words.
3. Write eight hundred ninety-four thousand, twenty-six using numerals.	**4.** Write six hundred twenty-two and thirty-seven hundredths using numerals.
5. What decimal is equivalent to $\frac{3}{11}$?	**6.** What decimal is equivalent to $\frac{7}{8}$?
7. Write 0.68 as a fraction in simplest form.	**8.** Write 0.762 as a fraction in simplest form.
9. Round 8,647 to the hundreds place.	**10.** Round 68.6423 to the hundredths place.
11. Round 890,164 to the thousands place.	**12.** Round 11.3972 to the tenths place.

94

Basic Computation Series 2000: Quizzes and Tests

Copyright © Dale Seymour Publications®

Place Value and Rounding

1. Write 59,647 in words.	**2.** Write 8,674.93 in words.
3. Write ninety-seven thousand sixty-six using numerals.	**4.** Write two hundred two and ninety-eight thousandths using numerals.
5. What decimal is equivalent to $\frac{5}{7}$?	**6.** What decimal is equivalent to $\frac{5}{6}$?
7. Write 0.94 as a fraction in simplest form.	**8.** Write 0.765 as a fraction in simplest form.
9. Round 54,894.22 to the thousands place.	**10.** Round 543.842 to the tenths place.
11. Round 8,033.4 to the hundreds place.	**12.** Round 473.8425 to the ones place.

Place Value and Rounding

1. Write 9,864 in words.	**2.** Write 574.807 in words.
3. Write nine thousand, six hundred two and eight hundredths using numerals.	**4.** Write five hundred thousand, and five thousandths using numerals.
5. What decimal is equivalent to $\frac{8}{9}$?	**6.** What decimal is equivalent to $\frac{15}{16}$?
7. Write 0.32 as a fraction in simplest form.	**8.** Write 0.375 as a fraction in simplest form.
9. Round 98.437 to the tenths place.	**10.** Round 649.8734 to the tens place.
11. Round 800.379 to the ones place.	**12.** Round 89.4372 to the hundredths place.

NAME

DATE

Ordering and Addition of Decimals

1. Circle the greatest number.	2. Circle the least number.	3. Circle the number closest to 85.
72.3 5.14169 13.00007 6.21 8.345	1.007 13.6 5 12.62 81.345	8.514 82.371 185.0 96.7 285.397

Find each sum.

4.   6.007
          8.21
  + 13.67
	5. 42.37
	          0.83
	          0.046
	   + 27
		6. Find the sum of 6.07, 0.0082, 8.6, and 9.

7. Add 63.47, 0.82, and 0.095.	8. Add 7.63, 0.0307, 8.2, and 19.	9. 175.6
		          0.083
		          0.0054
		   + 93

10. Find the sum of 16.053 and 182.4491.	11. Find the sum of 62.83, 0.97, 0.08, and 300.	12. Add 0.007, 0.092, 13.956, 0.812, and 367.835.

Ordering and Addition of Decimals

1. Circle the greatest number.	2. Circle the least number.	3. Circle the number closest to 175.
3.25 7.1499983 12.1 11.23976 46	53.004 12.376 2.10039 14.98 1.3989	17.503 95.175 163.9987 275.3 43.62

Find each sum.

4.   5.003
       6.94
+ 17.7096
	5. 38.03
	      0.98
	      0.016
	+ 12
		6. Find the sum of 4.07, 0.0059, 3.6, and 76.

7. Add 69.31, 0.63, and 0.953.	8. Add 5.83, 0.0606, 3.5, and 95.	9. 137.55
		      0.046
		      0.0039
		+ 58

10. Find the sum of 12.703 and 174.4466.	11. Find the sum of 58.37, 0.89, 0.30, and 7.	12. Add 0.006, 0.053, 14.006, 0.116, and 537.95.

Ordering and Addition of Decimals

1. Circle the greatest number.		**2.** Circle the least number.		**3.** Circle the number closest to 150.	
4.75	3.9	59.807	12.1	15.15	1,500
7.14998	0.03	3.79566	14	150.15	215.15
12.4	6.999989	1.3874	7.6	157	1,150.5

Find each sum.

4. 3.004 7.83 + 12.169	**5.** 39.04 0.98 0.016 + 25	**6.** Find the sum of 3.09, 0.0093, 5.9, and 34.
7. 49.52 + 0.68 + 0.68 = ?	**8.** 4.98 + 0.0405 + 5.8 = ?	**9.** 193.66 0.069 0.0027 + 87
10. Find the sum of 13.904 and 154.3386.	**11.** Add 783.85, 0.93, and 0.06.	**12.** Add 0.006, 0.068, 14.862, 0.113, and 342.981.

Ordering and Addition of Decimals

1. Circle the greatest number.	2. Circle the least number.	3. Circle the number closest to 55.
55.7 3.54721	58 0.614	5.56821 58.3
0.0012 142.95	0.00012 45.3	36.9 155.2
68.814	82.17	505.5

Find each sum.

4. 8.621	5. Find the sum of 0.92,	6. 3.678
29.6	9.2, and 92.	29.45
513		0.812
+ 0.473		503.4
		+ 2.57

7. Add 49, 4.9, 49.4, and 494.	8. Add 4.83, 0.376, 0.42, and 95.	9. 0.034
		2.05
		200.7
		+ 0.34

10. Find the sum of 57.302 and 136.09	11. 3.72 + 0.487 + 9 = ?	12. Add 35.92, 0.68, 0.006, 30, and 3.1402.

Subtraction of Decimals

Find each difference.

1. $\quad$ 9,573.28 $\quad$ $-$ $\quad$ 784.93	**2.** 936.42 $-$ 78.98 $=$?	**3.** How much less than 198 is 0.073?
4. Find the difference between 795.3 and 39.7.	**5.** $\quad$ 27.89 $\quad$ $-$ $\quad$ 0.0097	**6.** $\quad$ 58.007 $\quad$ $-$ 38.978
7. 3,000 $-$ 587.63 $=$?	**8.** $\quad$ 167.08 $\quad$ $-$ 13.098	**9.** How much greater than 83.75 is 1,900?
10. $\quad$ 187.66 $\quad$ $-$ 107.975	**11.** Find the difference between 15.96 and 7.038.	**12.** 3,897.02 $-$ 958.79 $=$?

Subtraction of Decimals

Find each difference.

1. How much less than 46.032 is 1.00727?	**2.** 0.50903 − 0.376212	**3.** Find the difference between 372.483 and 297.697.
4. 352.70004 − 272.83009	**5.** How much greater than 6.4572 is 13?	**6.** 43.5012 − 22.83
7. 727.301 − 452.326	**8.** 57.251 − 29.35721 = ?	**9.** How much less than 235 is 187.23?
10. 20.531 − 19.4832	**11.** Find the difference between 51 and 18.5239.	**12.** 1,000 − 847.2935 = ?

Subtraction of Decimals

Find each difference.

1. 329.63 − 143.94	**2.** Find the difference between 86.698 and 41.602.	**3.** 0.95317 − 0.42632
4. How much greater than 603.704 is 704.321?	**5.** 36,514.2 − 4,217.163	**6.** 8.4004 − 6.8216
7. 65.426 − 36.7 = ?	**8.** 33.0408 − 12.706	**9.** How much less than 72 is 36.438?
10. Find the difference between 234 and 0.456.	**11.** 2,436.81 − 946.026 = ?	**12.** 26,058.315 − 12,656.808

Subtraction of Decimals

Find each difference.

1. 8,434.62 − 846.35	**2.** 419.62 − 38.64 = ?	**3.** How much less than 170 is 0.035?

4. Find the difference between 895.4 and 27.6.	**5.** 39.87
	   − 0.0092
		6. 48.007
		   − 43.928

7. 2,000 − 876.93 = ?	**8.** 148.06 − 17.085	**9.** How much greater than 79.83 is 1,495?
10. Find the difference between 14.38 and 7.069.	**11.** 3,487.02 − 876.89 = ?	**12.** 42,735.095 − 712.874

Multiplication of Decimals

Find each product.

1. $\begin{array}{r} 3.59 \\ \times\ 4.2 \\ \hline \end{array}$	**2.** Find the product of 28.7 and 3.5.	**3.** $\begin{array}{r} 0.173 \\ \times\ 0.66 \\ \hline \end{array}$
4. Find the product of 75 and 7.92.	**5.** $69.4 \times 0.073 = ?$	**6.** $8.75 \times 4.016 = ?$
7. Multiply 78 and 8.7.	**8.** Find the product of 5.82 and 0.60.	**9.** $\begin{array}{r} 90.73 \\ \times\ 0.49 \\ \hline \end{array}$
10. $8.02 \times 44 = ?$	**11.** Multiply 0.48 and 0.35.	**12.** $5.866 \times 730 = ?$

Multiplication of Decimals

Find each product.

1.   2.37
     $\times$ 4.3
	2. Find the product of
	37.6 and 4.2.
		3. 0.173
		     $\times$ 0.44

4. Find the product of 73 and 9.32.	**5.** 46.7 $\times$ 0.083 = ?	**6.** Multiply 7.92 and 2.016.

7.   7.9
     $\times$ 9.3
	8. Find the product of
	4.72 and 0.30.
		9. 12.62
		     $\times$ 0.48

10. 9.06 $\times$ 33 = ?	**11.** Multiply 0.47 and 0.85.	**12.** 4.976 $\times$ 0.760 = ?

Multiplication of Decimals

Find each product.

1.   5.36
     $\times$ 4.2
	2. Find the product of
	     18.2 and 0.76.
		3. 0.436
		     $\times$ 0.312

4. Find the product of 745 and 2.8.	**5.** $0.643 \times 2.51 = ?$	**6.** Multiply 3.642 by 4.7.

7.   23.4
     $\times$ 32
	8. Find the product of
	     43.6 and 10.7.
		9. 32.4
		     $\times$ 0.612

10. $63.5 \times 17 = ?$	**11.** Multiply 0.3527 and 0.6.	**12.** Find the product of 3.65 and 1,000.

Multiplication of Decimals

Find each product.

1.   6.32
   × 2.7
	2. Find the product of
	    67.82 and 0.27.
		3. 49.37
		   × 3.09

4. Find the product of 92.8 and 101.2.	**5.** 873.1 × 0.033 = ?	**6.** Multiply 997.3 and 0.85.

7.   8.26
   × 72.7
	8. Find the product of
	    62.7 and 32.9.
		9. 7.53
		   × 12.9

10. 92.3 × 0.29 = ?	**11.** 0.7621
	   × 0.032
		12. Find the product of 659
		    and 0.62.

Division of Decimals

Find each quotient.

1. $6\overline{)0.5412}$	**2.** Divide 8.1341 by 0.13.	**3.** $0.8\overline{)12.288}$
4. Write $\frac{1}{8}$ in decimal form.	**5.** $5\overline{)0.68735}$	**6.** $\dfrac{458.2}{31.6} = ?$
7. $0.034\overline{)0.29648}$	**8.** Divide 11 by 0.025.	**9.** Write $\frac{7}{16}$ in decimal form.
10. $5.372 \div 0.34 = ?$	**11.** $0.07\overline{)0.11578}$	**12.** Divide 0.020319 by 0.0013.

Division of Decimals

Find each quotient.

1. $7\overline{)0.4207}$	**2.** Divide 0.3696 by 0.16.	**3.** $0.6\overline{)3.9246}$
4. Write $\frac{3}{8}$ in decimal form.	**5.** $5\overline{)0.68395}$	**6.** $\dfrac{889.22}{34.6} = ?$
7. $0.043\overline{)2.81263}$	**8.** Divide 9 by 0.075.	**9.** Write $\frac{5}{16}$ as a decimal.
10. $4.0544 \div 0.32 =$	**11.** $0.08\overline{)0.013912}$	**12.** Divide 0.024962 by 0.0014.

Division of Decimals

Find each quotient.

1. $9\overline{)0.6309}$	**2.** Divide 5.135 by 0.13.	**3.** $0.7\overline{)5.558}$
4. Write $\frac{7}{8}$ in decimal form.	**5.** $5\overline{)0.38935}$	**6.** $\dfrac{352.08}{32.6} = ?$
7. $0.029\overline{)1.3485}$	**8.** Divide 12 by 0.075.	**9.** Write $\frac{9}{16}$ in decimal form.
10. $19.832 \div 0.37 = ?$	**11.** $0.08\overline{)0.06432}$	**12.** Divide 0.54250 by 0.0014.

Division of Decimals

Find each quotient.

1. $7\overline{)0.476}$	**2.** Divide 0.5684 by 0.014.	**3.** $0.3\overline{)3.0609}$
4. Write $\frac{5}{8}$ in decimal form.	**5.** $0.42\overline{)84.042}$	**6.** $\dfrac{100.302}{0.006} = ?$
7. $0.0015\overline{)0.3075}$	**8.** Divide 1.6 by 0.008.	**9.** Write $\frac{11}{16}$ in decimal form.
10. $273.012 \div 0.30 = ?$	**11.** $0.04\overline{)33.36}$	**12.** Divide 2 by 0.005.

Operations with Decimals

Find each sum, difference, product, or quotient.

1. Add 6,932.17 and 2,734.66.	**2.** $\quad\quad$ 8.9112 $\quad\quad$ 67.543 $\quad\quad$ 2.66 $+$ 1,077.5614	**3.** Add 6.21, 27.3, and 867.223.
4. $\quad$ 1,003.32 $-\quad$ 627.401	**5.** $\quad$ 891.28 $-\quad$ 67.39	**6.** Subtract 27.697 from 866.4.
7. $\quad$ 2.7741 $\times\quad$ 2.34	**8.** $\quad$ 3.664 $\times\quad$ 3.01	**9.** $\quad$ 967.55 $\times\quad$ 0.22
10. $7.9\overline{)75.445}$	**11.** $56.7\overline{)114.0237}$	**12.** $21.9\overline{)1,997.28}$

Operations with Decimals

Find each sum, difference, product, or quotient.

1. Add 27.2739 and 793.21.	**2.** 4.003
	   29.68
	  472.622
	+ 4.0773
		3. Add 10.11, 87.3, and 100.76.

4. 84.6928 − 61.9989	**5.** 467.22 − 11.85	**6.** Subtract 47.881 from 756.92.
7. 7.32 × 2.44	**8.** 29.56 × 4.12	**9.** 97.21 × 0.66
10. $3.9\overline{)25.155}$	**11.** $72.9\overline{)219.5748}$	**12.** $21.3\overline{)1{,}393.02}$

Operations with Decimals

Find each sum, difference, product, or quotient.

1. Add 46.1085 and 3.279.	**2.** 8.512
	   64.11
	    2.567
	+ 804.72
		3. Add 4.32, 69.7, and 7,077.21.

4. 742.862 − 64.98	**5.** 27.87 − 24.985	**6.** Subtract 63.285 from 751.69.
7. 4.15 × 2.13	**8.** 7.26 × 8.05	**9.** 947.06 × 0.88
10. $3.1\overline{)22.072}$	**11.** $87.3\overline{)174.6873}$	**12.** $17.4\overline{)1,325.88}$

Operations with Decimals

Find each sum, difference, product, or quotient.

1. Add 59.6723 and 2.712.	**2.** $\begin{array}{r} 6.314 \\ 82.95 \\ 3.002 \\ +\,905.81 \\ \hline \end{array}$	**3.** Add 8.35, 72.8, and 1,004.675.
4. $\begin{array}{r} 937.621 \\ -\,59.28 \\ \hline \end{array}$	**5.** $\begin{array}{r} 43.96 \\ -\,12.858 \\ \hline \end{array}$	**6.** Subtract 54.372 from 836.54.
7. $\begin{array}{r} 3.14 \\ \times\,3.25 \\ \hline \end{array}$	**8.** $\begin{array}{r} 52.7 \\ \times\,70.5 \\ \hline \end{array}$	**9.** $\begin{array}{r} 827.6 \\ \times\,0.92 \\ \hline \end{array}$
10. $2.6\overline{)21.19}$	**11.** $92.7\overline{)98.1693}$	**12.** $14.6\overline{)1{,}214.72}$

Word Problems

Solve each problem.

1. The Teshara family spent the following amounts for food during a six week period: $100.61, $98.52, $85.00, $123.79, $116.86, and $95.48. How much did they spend for food during those six weeks?	**2.** Mrs. Swann owns a catering company that brought in $586.25, $1,186.90, $1,250.00, $1,585.75, $1,401.50 and $2,504.80 for the six working days of one week. What was the total amount brought in by the company?
3. A reservoir holds 53,633,200 gallons of water. This is 536.332 gallons for each person in the town. What is the population of the town?	**4.** Doma earned $15,805.14 during a year. She paid $2,516.43 in taxes. How much did she have left after taxes?
5. A farm yields 25.7 bushels of corn per acre. If 462.81 acres of corn were harvested, what was the total number of bushels of corn produced?	**6.** A city received 48.24 inches of rain during a year. What was the average amount of rainfall for each of the twelve months of the year?
7. A city vaccinated 2,300 animals for rabies. It used 1.26 cm^3 of vaccine for each animal. How much vaccine was used?	**8.** Mark allowed himself $3,500 for a trip to England. When he returned, he still had $486.15. How much did he spend on the trip?

Word Problems

Solve each problem.

---

1. A water tank has a volume of 1,200.5 cubic feet. The tank holds 8,979.74 gallons. How many gallons are in one cubic foot of water?

2. Mrs. Walker's interest-bearing checking account earned the following amounts over a five-month period: $89.16, $74.25, $101.60, $51.21, and $63.50. What was the total amount of interest earned during that period?

---

3. Travis uses 0.25 cups of salt for each gallon of water in his saltwater pond. If he needs 525 gallons of water to fill the pond, how much salt will he use?

4. The stock market dropped from 9,989.54 to 9,966.87. How much did the stock market drop?

---

5. Darrell can drive his car 756.5 miles on a tank of fuel. How far can he drive his car on 17.31 tanks of fuel?

6. Kirsten had $2,314.26 in her bank account at the beginning of the month. By the end of the month she had $863.58. How much did she spend?

---

7. Joanna returned from a fishing trip with five fish that weighed 1.2 pounds, 0.8 pounds, 3.6 pounds, 2.2 pounds, and 2.0 pounds. What was the total weight of the fish?

8. Lila ran 2,245.275 yards in 264.15 seconds. How many yards per second did she average?

Word Problems

Solve each problem.

1. Jim spent $12.49 for a shirt, $16.50 for jeans, and $68.35 for a jacket. Find the total cost of these items.	**2.** Ingrid has a bicycle shop. She collects sales tax which she sends to the state every four months. For the first four months of the year, she collected $452.73, $581.62, $385.41, and $481.05. How much did she collect?
3. Joe and Juan together sold $853.25 in raffle tickets for a fund raising project. Joe sold $385.79. How much did Juan sell?	**4.** The area of Rhode Island is 1,214 square miles. The population is about 900,000. To the nearest whole number, what is the average population per square mile?
5. Jose has a large ranch in Arizona. He has 2,347 calves to vaccinate. Each calf requires 1.57 cm^3 of vaccine. How much vaccine will be required?	**6.** Tina harvested an average of 48.2 bushels per acre of wheat from the 157.36 acres she planted. How many bushels of wheat did she harvest?
7. The distance by rail from Buffalo to New York City is 436.32 miles. The distance from Buffalo to Chicago is 510.1 miles. How much farther is it to Chicago than to New York City?	**8.** The area of Alaska is 585,412 square miles. The population is about 400,000. To the nearest hundredth, what is the average number of square miles per person?

Word Problems

Solve each problem.

---

1. The senior class held two fundraisers, a car wash and a bake sale. They made $526.15. If they made $227.50 on the car wash, how much did they make on the bake sale?

2. A class-action law suit was settled by paying a total of $4,995,000 to a group of 900,000 persons. How much money did each person receive if the money was equally divided?

3. Tasha earned the following amounts laying brick: $512.60, $425.50, $726.12, $900, and $327.67. What was the total amount she earned?

4. Arthur had $325 and spent $180.65. How much did he have left?

5. Ginny earned $123.16 each day for 27.5 days. What was her total earnings?

6. A gasoline tank on a car holds 19.6 gallons. The car averages 28.6 miles per gallon. How far can it travel on one tank of gasoline?

7. Julie jogged 3.4 miles on Saturday, 1.12 miles on Sunday, 2.58 miles on Monday and 5.03 miles on Tuesday. What was the total distance she jogged on these days?

8. The total land area of California is 156,361 square miles. California has a population of 22,000,000. To the nearest thousandth, what is the average number of square miles per person?

Percents

1. 4 is what percent of 5?	**2.** What percent of 12 is 6?	**3.** Write 0.62 as a percent.
4. Write $\frac{0.4}{100}$ as a percent.	**5.** Write $\frac{5}{8}$ as a percent.	**6.** Find 33% of 42.
7. Write 5.2% as a decimal.	**8.** 19 is 25% of what number?	**9.** Write 72% as a fraction in lowest terms.
10. Find $33\frac{1}{3}$% of 99.	**11.** Find 12% of 54.	**12.** What percent of the figure is shaded?

Percents

1. Write $\frac{3.5}{100}$ as a percent.	**2.** Find 16% of 68.	**3.** Write 0.0031 as a percent.
4. 15 is what percent of 20?	**5.** Write 84% as a fraction in lowest terms.	**6.** Find 9.2% of 16.
7. Write $\frac{7}{8}$ as a percent.	**8.** 24 is what percent of 20?	**9.** Write $\frac{5.7}{10}$ as a percent.
10. 45 is 75% of what number?	**11.** Write 17.5 as a percent.	**12.** What percent of the figure is shaded?

Percents

1. Write $\frac{2}{5}$ as a percent.	**2.** Write 0.16% as a decimal.	**3.** 4 is what percent of 5?
4. Find 17% of 63.	**5.** Write $\frac{0.51}{100}$ as a percent.	**6.** Find 30% of 80.
7. 27 is 25% of what number?	**8.** 20 is what percent of 50?	**9.** Find $12\frac{1}{2}$% of 104.
10. 7 is what percent of 35?	**11.** Write $\frac{7.6}{10}$ as a percent.	**12.** What percent of the figure is shaded?

Percents

1. Write $\frac{1}{4}$ as a percent.	**2.** Write 0.29 as a percent.	**3.** Write 43% as a decimal.
4. Write $\frac{30}{100}$ as a percent.	**5.** 20 is what percent of 100?	**6.** What number is 15% of 35?
7. Find 75% of 36.	**8.** 42 is $66\frac{2}{3}$% of what number?	**9.** 18 is what percent of 90?
10. Write $\frac{1.8}{10}$ as a percent.	**11.** Find 12.3% of 52.	**12.** What percent of the figure is shaded?

Word Problems

Solve each problem.

1. Find 20% of 135.	**2.** 35.69 is 43% of what number?
3. 13.12 is what percent of 82?	**4.** The regular price of a suit is $297. The suit is on sale for $33\frac{1}{3}$% off. Find the sale price.
5. A computer cost $1,500. It is on sale for $1,050. Find the rate of discount.	**6.** Dara borrowed $3,000. She was charged interest at 15% per year. Find the interest for one year.
7. The sale price of a pair of shoes is $21. This is 70% of the regular price. Find the regular price.	**8.** Guillermo paid $100 interest on money he borrowed for one year. The rate of interest was 10%. How much money did he borrow?
9. A bicycle is advertised for sale at a 20% discount. The regular price is $150. Find the sale price.	**10.** The cost of a house increased 12% in one year. The original cost was $50,000. Find the cost one year later.

Word Problems

Solve each problem.

1. Find 25% of 248.	**2.** 23.49 is 27% of what number?
3. 31.92 is what percent of 76?	**4.** The regular price of a suit is $224. The suit is on sale for $12\frac{1}{2}$% off. Find the sale price of the suit.
5. Quinton borrowed $2,500. He was charged interest at 12% per year. Find the amount of interest for one year.	**6.** A computer printer is regularly priced at $250. It is on sale for $200. Find the rate of discount.
7. The sale price of a pair of shoes is $30. This is 75% of the regular price. Find the regular price.	**8.** Carol paid $120 interest on money she borrowed for one year. The rate of interest was 8%. How much money did she borrow?
9. A bicycle is advertised for sale at a 25% discount. The regular price is $180. Find the sale price.	**10.** The cost of a house increased 13% in one year. The original cost was $75,000. Find the cost one year later.

Word Problems

Solve each problem.

1. Find $37\frac{1}{2}$% of 88.	**2.** 25.92 is 36% of what number?
3. 41.85 is what percent of 93?	**4.** The regular price of a suit is $448. The suit is on sale for 25% off. Find the sale price of the suit.
5. A scanner is regularly priced at $260. It is on sale for $227.50. Find the rate of discount.	**6.** The sale price of a pair of shoes is $28. This is $66\frac{2}{3}$% of the regular price. Find the regular price.
7. Ted borrowed $3,200. He was charged interest at the rate of 9% per year. Find the interest for one year.	**8.** Nina paid $110 interest on money she borrowed for one year. The rate of interest was 5%. How much money did she borrow?
9. A bicycle is advertised for sale at a $33\frac{1}{3}$% discount. The regular price is $162. Find the sale price.	**10.** The cost of a house increased $12\frac{1}{2}$% in one year. The original cost was $84,000. Find the cost one year later.

Word Problems

Solve each problem.

1. Find $66\frac{2}{3}\%$ of 96.	**2.** 58.71 is 57% of what number?
3. 13.77 is what percent of 27?	**4.** The regular price of a suit is $300. The suit is on sale for 25% off. Find the sale price of the suit.
5. A computer monitor is regularly priced at $300. It is on sale for $200. Find the rate of discount.	**6.** Tony borrowed $4,300. He was charged interest at the rate of 11% per year. Find the interest for one year.
7. The sale price of a pair of shoes is $35. This is $62\frac{1}{2}\%$ of the regular price. Find the regular price.	**8.** Jessie paid $140 interest on money she borrowed for one year. The rate of interest was 7%. How much money did she borrow?
9. A bicycle is advertised for sale at a $12\frac{1}{2}\%$ discount. The regular price is $150. Find the sale price.	**10.** The cost of a house increased 15% in one year. The original cost was $90,000. Find the cost one year later.

Equivalent Measures

Complete.

1. 45 °C = _____ °F	**2.** 95 °F = _____ °C	**3.** 90 °C = _____ °F
4. 4 hr = _____ min	**5.** 42 days = _____ wk	**6.** 5 yr = _____ mo
7. 216 in. = _____ ft	**8.** 237,600 ft = _____ mi	**9.** 15 yd = _____ in.
10. 4,200 ft = _____ yd	**11.** 2 mi = _____ yd	**12.** 17 ft = _____ in.

Equivalent Measures

Complete.

1. 20 °C = _____ °F	**2.** 77 °F = _____ °C	**3.** 80 °C = _____ °F
4. 7 yr = _____ mo	**5.** 408 hr = _____ days	**6.** 192 mo = _____ yr
7. 47 m = _____ cm	**8.** 26 km = _____ m	**9.** 301 mm = _____ cm
10. 32 m = _____ mm	**11.** 520 cm = _____ m	**12.** 17 mm = _____ m

Equivalent Measures

Complete.

1. 35 °C = _____ °F	**2.** 140 °F = _____ °C	**3.** 50 °C = _____ °F
4. 660 sec = _____ min	**5.** 5 hr = _____ min	**6.** 12 yr = _____ mo
7. 1,872 in. = _____ yd	**8.** 3 mi = _____ ft	**9.** 412 yd = _____ ft
10. 42 ft = _____ yd	**11.** 47 yd = _____ ft	**12.** 3 mi = _____ yd

Equivalent Measures

Complete.

1. 60 °C = _____ °F	**2.** 122 °F = _____ °C	**3.** 149 °F = _____ °C
4. 60 wk = _____ mo	**5.** 13 mo = _____ wk	**6.** 180 mo = _____ yr
7. 47 km = _____ m	**8.** 6,152 mm = _____ m	**9.** 83 cm = _____ km
10. 0.59 cm = _____ mm	**11.** 63.5 m = _____ km	**12.** 82 mm = _____ m

Measuring Angles

Use a protractor to measure each angle.

1. $m\angle A =$ _____

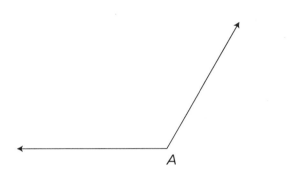

2. $m\angle B =$ _____

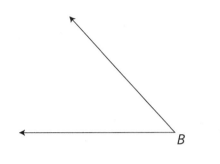

3. $m\angle C =$ _____

$m\angle D =$ _____

$m\angle E =$ _____

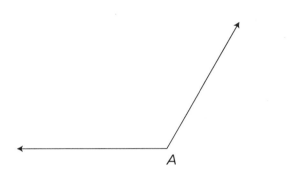

4. $m\angle F =$ _____

$m\angle G =$ _____

$m\angle H =$ _____

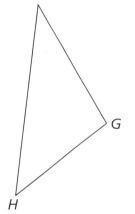

5. $m\angle J =$ _____

$m\angle K =$ _____

$m\angle L =$ _____

$m\angle M =$ _____

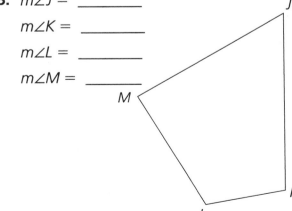

6. $m\angle N =$ _____

$m\angle O =$ _____

$m\angle P =$ _____

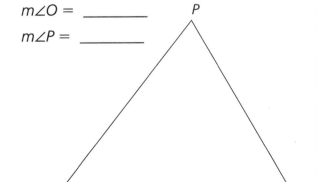

Measuring Angles

Use a protractor to measure each angle.

1. m∠A = _____

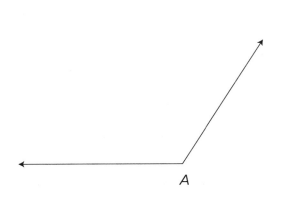

2. m∠B = _____

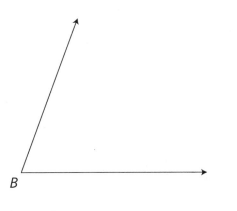

3. m∠C = _____
m∠D = _____
m∠E = _____

4. m∠F = _____
m∠G = _____
m∠H = _____

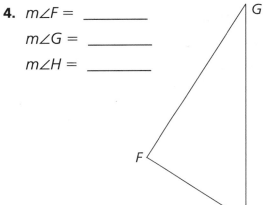

5. m∠J = _____
m∠K = _____
m∠L = _____

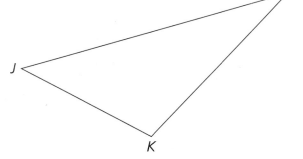

6. m∠M = _____
m∠N = _____
m∠O = _____
m∠P = _____

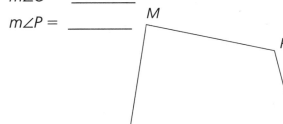

Measuring Angles

Use a protractor to measure each angle.

1. $m\angle A =$ _____

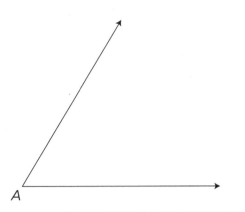

2. $m\angle B =$ _____

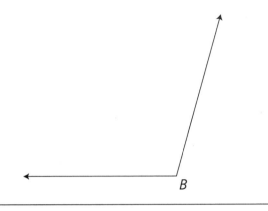

3. $m\angle C =$ _____
$m\angle D =$ _____
$m\angle E =$ _____

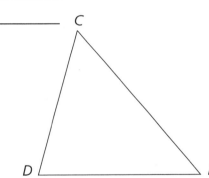

4. $m\angle F =$ _____
$m\angle G =$ _____
$m\angle H =$ _____

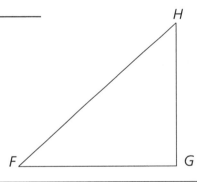

5. $m\angle J =$ _____
$m\angle K =$ _____
$m\angle L =$ _____
$m\angle M =$ _____

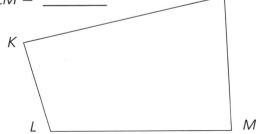

6. $m\angle N =$ _____
$m\angle O =$ _____
$m\angle P =$ _____

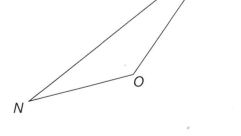

Measuring Angles

Use a protractor to measure each angle.

1. m∠A = _____

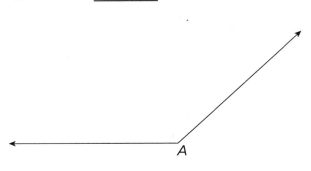

2. m∠B = _____

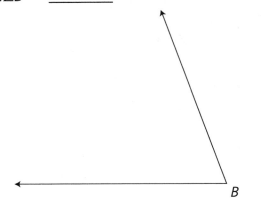

3. m∠C = _____
　　m∠D = _____
　　m∠E = _____

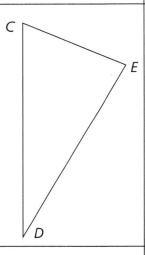

4. m∠F = _____
　　m∠G = _____
　　m∠H = _____

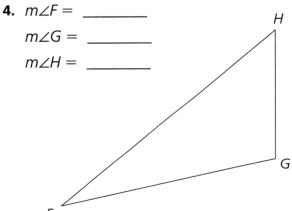

5. m∠J = _____
　　m∠K = _____
　　m∠L = _____

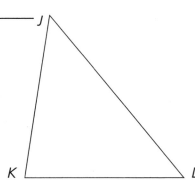

6. m∠M = _____
　　m∠N = _____
　　m∠O = _____
　　m∠P = _____

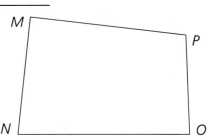

Area and Perimeter of Rectangles

For each problem, find the area and perimeter of a rectangle with the given dimensions. Be sure to include units in your answers.

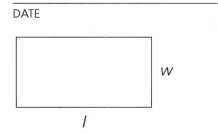

w

l

	l	w	Area	Perimeter
1.	$2\frac{1}{2}$ in.	$1\frac{1}{4}$ in.		
2.	2 yd	1 yd		
3.	$2\frac{1}{2}$ ft	2 ft		
4.	$3\frac{1}{2}$ in.	$3\frac{1}{2}$ in.		
5.	$2\frac{1}{4}$ mi	$1\frac{1}{4}$ mi		

Area and Perimeter of Rectangles

For each problem, find the area and perimeter of a rectangle with the given dimensions. Be sure to include units in your answers.

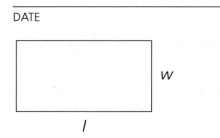

	l	*w*	Area	Perimeter
1.	2.5 m	1.5 m		
2.	2.25 km	1 km		
3.	1.75 dm	1.75 dm		
4.	4.25 m	1.25 m		
5.	5.25 cm	1.5 cm		

Area and Perimeter of Rectangles

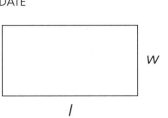

For each problem, find the area and perimeter of a rectangle with the given dimensions. Write answers in simplest form. Be sure to include units in your answers.

l	*w*	Area	Perimeter
1. $5\frac{1}{2}$ in.	$1\frac{1}{4}$ in.		
2. $2\frac{3}{4}$ mi	2 mi		
3. 3 ft	$1\frac{1}{2}$ ft		
4. $3\frac{1}{4}$ yd	$1\frac{1}{2}$ yd		
5. 4 in.	$\frac{3}{4}$ in.		

Area and Perimeter of Rectangles

For each problem, find the area and perimeter of a rectangle with the given dimensions. Be sure to include units in your answers.

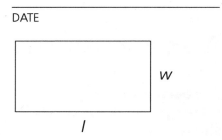

	l	*w*	Area	Perimeter
1.	2.5 km	1.75 km		
2.	2 dm	1.25 dm		
3.	3.75 m	2.25 m		
4.	2.5 km	1.4 km		
5.	4.25 cm	1 cm		

Triangles, Parallelograms, and Trapezoids

Measure the length of the sides and the altitude of each figure to the nearest quarter-inch. Then find the area (*A*) and perimeter (*P*) of each figure. Write answers in simplest form. Be sure to include units in your answers.

1. $a =$ _____

$b =$ _____

$c =$ _____

$h =$ _____

$A =$ _____

$P =$ _____

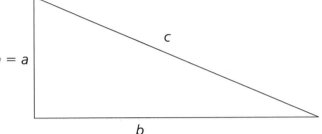

2. $a =$ _____

$b_1 =$ _____

$b_2 =$ _____

$c =$ _____

$h =$ _____

$A =$ _____

$P =$ _____

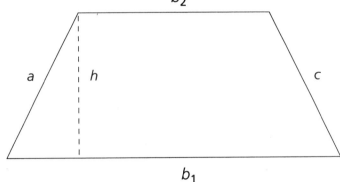

3. $a =$ _____

$b =$ _____

$h =$ _____

$A =$ _____

$P =$ _____

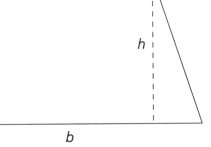

Triangles, Parallelograms, and Trapezoids

Measure the length of the sides and the altitude of each figure to the nearest millimeter. Then find the area (*A*) and perimeter (*P*) of each figure. Be sure to include units in your answers.

1. $a =$ _____

$b =$ _____

$c =$ _____

$h =$ _____

$A =$ _____

$P =$ _____

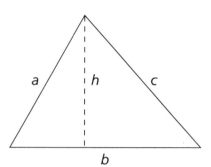

2. $a =$ _____

$b =$ _____

$h =$ _____

$A =$ _____

$P =$ _____

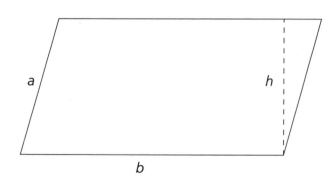

3. $a =$ _____

$b_1 =$ _____

$b_2 =$ _____

$c =$ _____

$h =$ _____

$A =$ _____

$P =$ _____

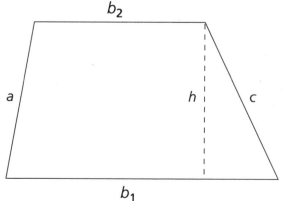

Triangles, Parallelograms, and Trapezoids

Measure the length of the sides and the altitude of each figure to the nearest quarter-inch. Then find the area (*A*) and perimeter (*P*) of each figure. Write answers in simplest form. Be sure to include units in your answers.

1. $a =$ _____
$b =$ _____
$h =$ _____
$A =$ _____
$P =$ _____

2. $a =$ _____
$c =$ _____
$h =$ _____
$A =$ _____
$P =$ _____

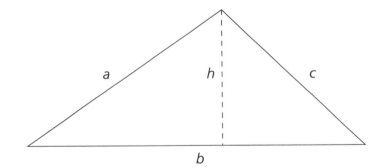

3. $a =$ _____
$b_1 =$ _____
$b_2 =$ _____
$c =$ _____
$h =$ _____
$A =$ _____
$P =$ _____

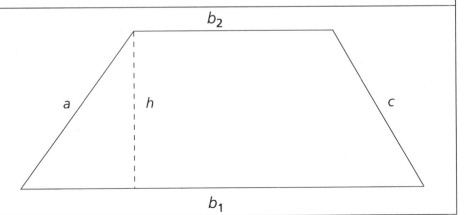

Triangles, Parallelograms, and Trapezoids

Measure the length of the sides and the altitude of each figure to the nearest millimeter. Then find the area (*A*) and perimeter (*P*) of each figure. Be sure to include units in your answers.

1. $a =$ _____

$b =$ _____

$c =$ _____

$h =$ _____

$A =$ _____

$P =$ _____

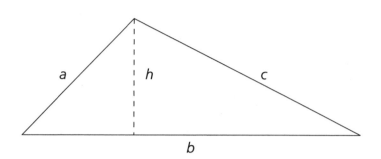

2. $a =$ _____

$b =$ _____

$h =$ _____

$A =$ _____

$P =$ _____

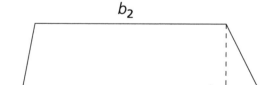

3. $a =$ _____

$b_1 =$ _____

$b_2 =$ _____

$c =$ _____

$h =$ _____

$A =$ _____

$P =$ _____

Surface Area and Volume

Find the surface area and volume of each shape. Use 3.14 for π. Be sure to include units in your answers.

1. Cube 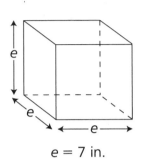 $e = 7$ in.	**2.** Rectangular Prism 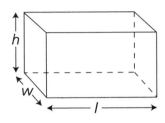 $l = 25$ ft $w = 17$ ft $h = 13$ ft	**3.** Cylinder 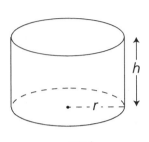 $r = 38$ in. $h = 13$ in.
Surface Area = _____ Volume = _____	Surface Area = _____ Volume = _____	Surface Area = _____ Volume = _____

Find the volume of each shape. Use 3.14 for π. Be sure to include units in your answers.

4. Triangular Prism 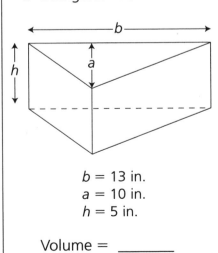 $b = 13$ in. $a = 10$ in. $h = 5$ in.	**5.** Sphere 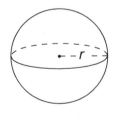 $r = 45$ ft	**6.** Cone 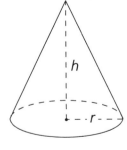 $r = 150$ in. $h = 85$ in.
Volume = _____	Volume = _____	Volume = _____

Surface Area and Volume

Find the surface area and volume of each shape. Use 3.14 for π. Be sure to include units in your answers.

1. Cube	2. Rectangular Prism	3. Cylinder
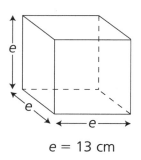	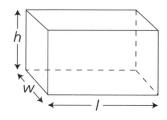	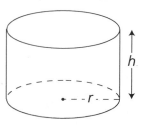
e = 13 cm	l = 17 mm w = 8 mm h = 6 mm	r = 14 cm h = 12 cm
Surface Area = _____ Volume = _____	Surface Area = _____ Volume = _____	Surface Area = _____ Volume = _____

Find the volume of each shape. Use 3.14 for π. Be sure to include units in your answers.

4. Triangular Prism	5. Sphere	6. Cone
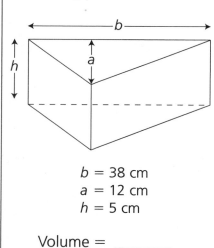	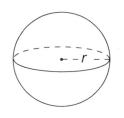	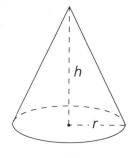
b = 38 cm a = 12 cm h = 5 cm	r = 21 m	r = 29 mm h = 12 mm
Volume = _____	Volume = _____	Volume = _____

Surface Area and Volume

Find the surface area and volume of each shape. Use 3.14 for π. Be sure to include units in your answers.

1. Cube	**2.** Rectangular Prism	**3.** Cylinder
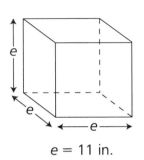	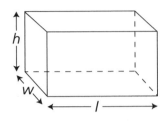	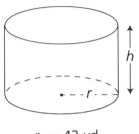
e = 11 in.	l = 16 ft w = 9 ft h = 3 ft	r = 42 yd h = 28 yd
Surface Area = _____ Volume = _____	Surface Area = _____ Volume = _____	Surface Area = _____ Volume = _____

Find the volume of each shape. Use 3.14 for π. Be sure to include units in your answers.

4. Triangular Prism	**5.** Sphere	**6.** Cone
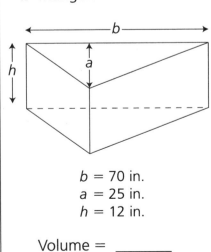	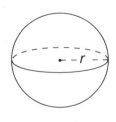	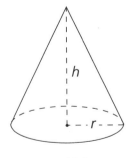
b = 70 in. a = 25 in. h = 12 in.	r = 35 in.	r = 49 in. h = 27 in.
Volume = _____	Volume = _____	Volume = _____

Copyright © Dale Seymour Publications®

Surface Area and Volume

Find the surface area and volume of each shape. Use 3.14 for π. Be sure to include units in your answers.

1. Cube	**2.** Rectangular Prism	**3.** Cylinder
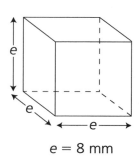	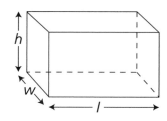	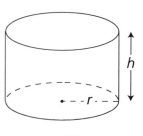
$e = 8$ mm	$l = 35$ cm $w = 22$ cm $h = 8$ cm	$r = 28$ cm $h = 9$ cm
Surface Area = _____ Volume = _____	Surface Area = _____ Volume = _____	Surface Area = _____ Volume = _____

Find the volume of each shape. Use 3.14 for π. Be sure to include units in your answers.

4. Triangular Prism	**5.** Sphere	**6.** Cone
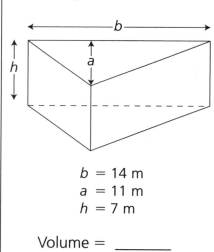	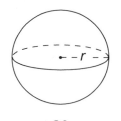	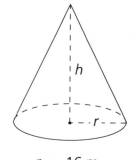
$b = 14$ m $a = 11$ m $h = 7$ m	$r = 30$ cm	$r = 16$ m $h = 15$ m
Volume = _____	Volume = _____	Volume = _____

Circles

Find the radius (*r*), circumference (*C*), and area (*A*) of each circle given the measure of its diameter (*d*). Use 3.14 for π. Be sure to include units in your answers.

1. *d* = 50 in.

    r = _____

    C = _____

    A = _____

2. *d* = 38 ft

    r = _____

    C = _____

    A = _____

3. *d* = 4 yd

    r = _____

    C = _____

    A = _____

4. *d* = 30 ft

    r = _____

    C = _____

    A = _____

5. *d* = 15 in.

    r = _____

    C = _____

    A = _____

Circles

Find the radius (*r*), circumference (*C*), and area (*A*) of each circle given the measure of its diameter (*d*). Use 3.14 for π. Be sure to include units in your answers.

1. *d* = 34 mm

   r = _____

   C = _____

   A = _____

2. *d* = 40 cm

   r = _____

   C = _____

   A = _____

3. *d* = 20 dm

   r = _____

   C = _____

   A = _____

4. *d* = 36 m

   r = _____

   C = _____

   A = _____

5. *d* = 19 cm

   r = _____

   C = _____

   A = _____

Circles

Find the radius (*r*), circumference (*C*), and area (*A*) of each circle given the measure of its diameter (*d*). Use 3.14 for π. Be sure to include units in your answers.

1. *d* = 10 yd

   r = _____

   C = _____

   A = _____

2. *d* = 32 in.

   r = _____

   C = _____

   A = _____

3. *d* = 18 ft

   r = _____

   C = _____

   A = _____

4. *d* = 52 in.

   r = _____

   C = _____

   A = _____

5. *d* = 45 ft

   r = _____

   C = _____

   A = _____

Circles

Find the radius (*r*), circumference (*C*), and area (*A*) of each circle given the measure of its diameter (*d*). Use 3.14 for π. Be sure to include units in your answers.

1. *d* = 5 km

   r = _____

   C = _____

   A = _____

2. *d* = 60 mm

   r = _____

   C = _____

   A = _____

3. *d* = 14 dm

   r = _____

   C = _____

   A = _____

4. *d* = 76 cm

   r = _____

   C = _____

   A = _____

5. *d* = 25 m

   r = _____

   C = _____

   A = _____

Money

Each purchase is to be taken out of $20. Determine the most efficient change.

1. Purchase: $9.72	**2.** Purchase: $16.81	**3.** Purchase: $12.57
_____ $10 _____ 25¢ _____ $ 5 _____ 10¢ _____ $ 1 _____ 5¢ _____ 1¢	_____ $10 _____ 25¢ _____ $ 5 _____ 10¢ _____ $ 1 _____ 5¢ _____ 1¢	_____ $10 _____ 25¢ _____ $ 5 _____ 10¢ _____ $ 1 _____ 5¢ _____ 1¢
4. Purchase: $8.32	**5.** Purchase: $5.16	**6.** Purchase: $7.78
_____ $10 _____ 25¢ _____ $ 5 _____ 10¢ _____ $ 1 _____ 5¢ _____ 1¢	_____ $10 _____ 25¢ _____ $ 5 _____ 10¢ _____ $ 1 _____ 5¢ _____ 1¢	_____ $10 _____ 25¢ _____ $ 5 _____ 10¢ _____ $ 1 _____ 5¢ _____ 1¢

Find the unit price of each item. Then circle the best buy.

7. a. $1.43 for 13 oz	**8. a.** $29.95 for a box of 25	**9. a.** $4.48 for 16 lb
b. $2.34 for 18 oz	**b.** $60.50 for a box of 50	**b.** $11.25 for 45 lb
c. $3.36 for 32 oz	**c.** $118.00 for a box of 100	**c.** $14.04 for 52 lb
10. a. $8.96 for 16 gal	**11. a.** $1.04 for 13 oz	**12. a.** $2.25 for 25 ft
b. $23.84 for 42 gal	**b.** $3.24 for 27 oz	**b.** $8.00 for 100 ft
c. $35.40 for 60 gal	**c.** $3.64 for 52 oz	**c.** $10.00 for 200 ft

Money

Each purchase is to be taken out of $20. Determine the most efficient change.

1. Purchase: $7.32	**2.** Purchase: $15.57	**3.** Purchase: $12.59
_____ $10 _____ 25¢	_____ $10 _____ 25¢	_____ $10 _____ 25¢
_____ $ 5 _____ 10¢	_____ $ 5 _____ 10¢	_____ $ 5 _____ 10¢
_____ $ 1 _____ 5¢	_____ $ 1 _____ 5¢	_____ $ 1 _____ 5¢
_____ 1¢	_____ 1¢	_____ 1¢
4. Purchase: $3.68	**5.** Purchase: $9.83	**6.** Purchase: $7.97
_____ $10 _____ 25¢	_____ $10 _____ 25¢	_____ $10 _____ 25¢
_____ $ 5 _____ 10¢	_____ $ 5 _____ 10¢	_____ $ 5 _____ 10¢
_____ $ 1 _____ 5¢	_____ $ 1 _____ 5¢	_____ $ 1 _____ 5¢
_____ 1¢	_____ 1¢	_____ 1¢

Find the unit price of each item. Then circle the best buy.

7. a. $2.70 for 10 g	**8. a.** $3.75 for a box of 25	**9. a.** $2.32 for 8 kg
b. $3.15 for 15 g	**b.** $6.00 for a box of 50	**b.** $3.00 for 10 kg
c. $5.00 for 20 g	**c.** $10.00 for a box of 100	**c.** $4.80 for 15 kg
10. a. $7.65 for 15 mL	**11. a.** $1.76 for 8 L	**12. a.** $4.50 for 50 m
b. $13.75 for 25 mL	**b.** $2.88 for 12 L	**b.** $6.00 for 75 m
c. $22.40 for 40 mL	**c.** $4.20 for 20 L	**c.** $10.00 for 100 m

Money

Each purchase is to be taken out of $20. Determine the most efficient change.

1. Purchase: $12.49	**2.** Purchase: $7.83

1. Purchase: $12.49

_____ $10   _____ 25¢
_____ $ 5   _____ 10¢
_____ $ 1   _____ 5¢
              _____ 1¢

2. Purchase: $7.83

_____ $10   _____ 25¢
_____ $ 5   _____ 10¢
_____ $ 1   _____ 5¢
              _____ 1¢

3. Purchase: $16.48

_____ $10   _____ 25¢
_____ $ 5   _____ 10¢
_____ $ 1   _____ 5¢
              _____ 1¢

4. Purchase: $4.07

_____ $10   _____ 25¢
_____ $ 5   _____ 10¢
_____ $ 1   _____ 5¢
              _____ 1¢

5. Purchase: $8.52

_____ $10   _____ 25¢
_____ $ 5   _____ 10¢
_____ $ 1   _____ 5¢
              _____ 1¢

6. Purchase: $14.81

_____ $10   _____ 25¢
_____ $ 5   _____ 10¢
_____ $ 1   _____ 5¢
              _____ 1¢

Find the unit price of each item. Then circle the best buy.

7. a. $5.70 for 15 g

   b. $8.82 for 21 g

   c. $16.80 for 30 g

8. a. $3.00 for a box of 100

   b. $4.00 for a box of 200

   c. $7.50 for a box of 500

9. a. $3.00 for 25 m

   b. $8.25 for 75 m

   c. $18.00 for 200 m

10. a. $6.30 for 18 mL

    b. $7.44 for 24 mL

    c. $12.48 for 48 mL

11. a. $2.30 for 125 kg

    b. $3.40 for 200 kg

    c. $8.00 for 400 kg

12. a. $2.25 for 15 m

    b. $5.10 for 30 m

    c. $11.04 for 48 m

Money

Each purchase is to be taken out of $20. Determine the most efficient change.

1. Purchase: $11.58		2. Purchase: $13.32		3. Purchase: $17.82	
_____ $10	_____ 25¢	_____ $10	_____ 25¢	_____ $10	_____ 25¢
_____ $ 5	_____ 10¢	_____ $ 5	_____ 10¢	_____ $ 5	_____ 10¢
_____ $ 1	_____ 5¢	_____ $ 1	_____ 5¢	_____ $ 1	_____ 5¢
	_____ 1¢		_____ 1¢		_____ 1¢
4. Purchase: $9.28		5. Purchase: $7.85		6. Purchase: $9.61	
_____ $10	_____ 25¢	_____ $10	_____ 25¢	_____ $10	_____ 25¢
_____ $ 5	_____ 10¢	_____ $ 5	_____ 10¢	_____ $ 5	_____ 10¢
_____ $ 1	_____ 5¢	_____ $ 1	_____ 5¢	_____ $ 1	_____ 5¢
	_____ 1¢		_____ 1¢		_____ 1¢

Find the unit price of each item. Then circle the best buy.

7. a. $1.55 for 43	8. a. $4.14 for 23 oz	9. a. $4.55 for a box of 35
b. $2.82 for 91	b. $7.92 for 36 oz	b. $12.60 for a box of 90
c. $3.75 for 117	c. $9.88 for 52 oz	c. $15.40 for a box of 140
10. a. $1.20 for 75 in.^{2}	11. a. $0.77 for 35	12. a. $1.17 for 13 oz
b. $1.88 for 125 in.^{2}	b. $1.08 for 60	b. $2.16 for 27 oz
c. $2.31 for 165 in.^{2}	c. $2.10 for 100	c. $2.94 for 42 oz

Word Problems

Solve each problem.

---

1. A car dealer gave a $700 rebate on a $5,800 car. To the nearest whole number, what percent rebate was this?

---

2. If the heart pumps 80 mL of blood each second, how many liters of blood does it pump each hour?

---

3. A cheetah, the fastest animal on earth, can run 70 miles per hour. How many feet per second is this?

---

4. The wheel of a bicycle has a 26-inch diameter. Each time the wheel turns a complete revolution, the bicycle moves a distance equal to the circumference of the wheel. How far has a rider traveled when the wheel has gone around 1,000 times? (Use $\pi = 3.14$. Give your answer to the nearest foot.)

---

5. The population of Colorado was 3,407,209 one year. The state spent $7,598,076.07 on pollution control. What amount was spent per person?

---

6. At the sixty-eighth annual Millrose games, Francie Larrieu won the 1,000-yard run with a time of 2 minutes 27 seconds. How fast did she run in miles per hour? (Give your answer to the nearest tenth.)

Word Problems

Solve each problem.

---

1. During his career as a football player, Don Meredith attempted 2,308 passes and completed 1,170. To the nearest whole percent, what percent of his passes were incomplete?

---

2. There were 510 points possible in a mathematics class for the semester. If Leigh's grade was 90%, how many points had she missed during the semester?

---

3. Andreas worked 29 hours during the week at $7.57 per hour. Eighteen and one-half percent of his pay was withheld for social security, state disability insurance, and income tax. How much take-home pay did he receive?

---

4. Jolene's car gets 32 miles per gallon. She pays $1.56 per gallon for gasoline. How much did she spend for gasoline on a 2,600 mile trip?

---

5. A vat in the shape of a cylinder has radius 5 feet and height 7 feet. It is to be filled with cleaning fluid. The cleaning fluid costs $26.75 per gallon. What will it cost to fill the tank? (1 ft^3 = 7.48 gal. Use π = 3.14. Give your answer to the nearest dollar.)

---

6. Albert has 213 pine trees to be sprayed to control the pine beetle. Each gallon of spray concentrate costs $49.50 and mixes with water to make 40 gallons of diluted spray. It takes $\frac{3}{4}$ gallons of diluted spray for each tree. How much will it cost to spray all 213 trees? (Give your answer to the nearest dollar.)

Basic Computation Series 2000: Quizzes and Tests

Word Problems

Solve each problem.

---

1. Janice performed an experiment with her motorcycle at the local race track. In five tries it took 3.1 seconds, 3.0 seconds, 2.8 seconds, 3.6 seconds, and 2.9 seconds for her to accelerate to 20 miles per hour. What was the average time needed for the cycle to reach 20 miles per hour?

---

2. On a back-packing trip, Carlos walked 16 kilometers per day for each of five days. He walked a total of 50 hours. What was his average rate of walking in kilometers per hour?

---

3. The outside walls of a rectangular-shaped warehouse are to be painted. The warehouse is 100 meters long, 90 meters wide, and 30 meters high, and has no windows. One liter of paint covers 100 square meters. How many liters of paint will be needed?

---

4. Berta invested $2,500 for two years at simple interest. What rate of interest did she receive if her income over the two-year period was $700?

---

5. In one day of shopping, Rick spent $29.75 on clothes, $16.50 in the supermarket, and $14.00 at the bookstore. All of these items were taxed at 6%. How much money did he have left out of $75.00?

---

6. A new car costs $33,750. Sales tax is $6\frac{1}{2}$%, and the title and license together cost $173.50. What is the total cost of the car?

Word Problems

Solve each problem.

1. Li's grades on 10 tests were 83, 77, 96, 63, 89, 74, 80, 92, 67, and 81. What was the average of these grades?

2. Phil worked 40 hours at $8.75 an hour. He had deductions totaling $12.88. What was his net pay?

3. A coat bought on a 25% off sale costs $52.56. What was the original price of the coat?

4. A room measuring 25 feet by 18 feet is to be carpeted. If the price of the carpet is $12.50 per square yard, what will it cost to carpet the room?

5. Trudy bought 5 items costing $6.95, $5.27, $12.52, $6.81, and $23.17, respectively. She paid 6% sales tax on these items. What was the total bill, including tax?

6. Jorge drove his car 2,100 kilometers and bought gasoline six times. The amounts of his gasoline purchases were $17.52, $21.43, $18.47, $19.62, $15.43, and $20.76. What was the average cost of his fuel per kilometer? (Give your answer to the nearest cent.)

Semester Test 1, Form A

Work each problem. Then circle the letter of the best answer.

---

1. Add.

509
37
628
4
+ 283

A. 1,431   **B.** 1,441

C. 1,461   **D.** None of these

---

2. Find the sum of 695 and 8,321.

A. 9,016   **B.** 15,271

C. 8,916   **D.** 8,016

---

3. Find the total.

1,287
327
1,483
6,029
43
+ 7,705

A. 16,874   **B.** 16,854

C. 16,774   **D.** 15,874

---

4. Add.

9,011
7,562
3,881
+ 4,625

A. 25,089   **B.** 24,089

C. 25,079   **D.** None of these

---

5. Subtract.

8,057
− 392

A. 7,665   **B.** 3,421

C. 7,645   **D.** 7,765

---

6. Subtract 3,851 from 9,836.

A. 5,985   **B.** 6,015

C. 6,025   **D.** 6,085

Semester Test 1, Form A

Work each problem. Then circle the letter of the best answer.

7. 3,068 − 447 = ?	**A.** 2,521	**B.** 3,421
	C. 3,521	**D.** 2,621

8. Find the product of 67 and 53.	**A.** 3,531	**B.** 3,551
	C. 3,451	**D.** None of these

9. Multiply. $\begin{array}{r} 357 \\ \times\ 602 \\ \hline \end{array}$	**A.** 22,134	**B.** 214,904
	C. 216,114	**D.** 214,914

10. Multiply 608 by 275.	**A.** 167,180	**B.** 167,200
	C. 18,700	**D.** 179,200

11. Divide. $53\overline{)2,491}$	**A.** 407	**B.** 470
	C. 47	**D.** None of these

12. Divide 15,035 by 5.	**A.** 307	**B.** 301
	C. 3,001	**D.** 3,007

13. 13,626 ÷ 6 = ?	**A.** 2,301	**B.** 2,271
	C. 11,271	**D.** 22,071

14. Add. $\begin{array}{r} \frac{5}{12} \\ +\ \frac{5}{8} \\ \hline \end{array}$	**A.** $\frac{1}{2}$	**B.** $\frac{10}{20}$
	C. $\frac{25}{48}$	**D.** $1\frac{1}{24}$

Semester Test 1, Form A

Work each problem. Then circle the letter of the best answer.

---

15. Add $\frac{1}{4}$ and $\frac{5}{6}$.

A. $1\frac{1}{12}$ **B.** $\frac{6}{10}$

C. $\frac{3}{5}$ **D.** $\frac{13}{14}$

---

16. Find the sum of $\frac{4}{5}$ and $\frac{7}{15}$.

A. $1\frac{4}{15}$ **B.** $\frac{11}{20}$

C. $\frac{19}{30}$ **D.** None of these

---

17. Subtract $\frac{5}{8}$ from $\frac{7}{8}$.

A. $1\frac{1}{4}$ **B.** $\frac{1}{4}$

C. $1\frac{4}{8}$ **D.** $\frac{12}{16}$

---

18. Subtract $\frac{6}{7}$ from $\frac{11}{12}$.

A. $1\frac{25}{28}$ **B.** $\frac{8}{42}$

C. $\frac{4}{21}$ **D.** $\frac{5}{84}$

---

19. $\frac{4}{5} \times \frac{20}{21} = ?$

A. $\frac{4}{7}$ **B.** $\frac{20}{21}$

C. $\frac{16}{21}$ **D.** $\frac{100}{105}$

---

20. Find the least common denominator for $\frac{7}{20}$ and $\frac{17}{24}$.

A. 80   **B.** 60

C. 120   **D.** 100

---

21. $\frac{5}{6} - \frac{3}{5} = ?$

A. $\frac{7}{30}$ **B.** $1\frac{13}{30}$

C. $\frac{7}{60}$ **D.** $\frac{43}{60}$

---

22. $\frac{5}{12} \times \frac{10}{13} = ?$

A. $\frac{5}{26}$ **B.** $\frac{25}{78}$

C. $\frac{5}{13}$ **D.** None of these

Semester Test 1, Form A

Work each problem. Then circle the letter of the best answer.

23. $\frac{4}{9} \times \frac{15}{16} \times \frac{12}{25} = ?$	**A.** 5 **C.** $\frac{12}{15}$	**B.** $\frac{3}{5}$ **D.** $\frac{1}{5}$
24. Divide $\frac{8}{15}$ by 4.	**A.** $\frac{32}{15}$ **C.** $7\frac{1}{2}$	**B.** $\frac{15}{32}$ **D.** $\frac{2}{15}$
25. $\frac{5}{6} \div \frac{7}{12} = ?$	**A.** $\frac{5}{14}$ **C.** $1\frac{3}{7}$	**B.** $\frac{35}{72}$ **D.** None of these
26. $7 \div \frac{3}{7} = ?$	**A.** 3 **C.** $\frac{3}{49}$	**B.** $16\frac{1}{3}$ **D.** $\frac{1}{3}$
27. Add. $\qquad 12\frac{2}{7}$ $\qquad\qquad + 11\frac{3}{7}$	**A.** $23\frac{5}{14}$ **C.** $23\frac{5}{7}$	**B.** $23\frac{6}{49}$ **D.** $23\frac{1}{7}$
28. Add $18\frac{1}{8}$ and $6\frac{3}{8}$.	**A.** $24\frac{1}{4}$ **C.** $24\frac{1}{8}$	**B.** $24\frac{1}{2}$ **D.** $24\frac{5}{8}$
29. Find the sum of $17\frac{1}{4}$ and $12\frac{1}{3}$.	**A.** $29\frac{2}{7}$ **C.** 30	**B.** $29\frac{7}{12}$ **D.** $29\frac{1}{12}$
30. Add. $\qquad 8\frac{3}{5}$ $\qquad\qquad + 7\frac{2}{3}$	**A.** $16\frac{1}{2}$ **C.** $15\frac{2}{3}$	**B.** $15\frac{5}{8}$ **D.** $16\frac{4}{15}$

Semester Test 1, Form A

Work each problem. Then circle the letter of the best answer.

---

31. Find the sum of $6\frac{5}{8}$ and $9\frac{7}{12}$.

   A. $15\frac{5}{24}$ **B.** $15\frac{12}{16}$

   C. $16\frac{5}{24}$ **D.** $15\frac{3}{4}$

---

32. Add. $12\frac{1}{6}$

        $+\ 7\frac{1}{12}$

   A. $20\frac{8}{18}$ **B.** $20\frac{1}{2}$

   C. $19\frac{2}{3}$ **D.** $19\frac{1}{4}$

---

33. Subtract. $16\frac{6}{7}$

         $-\ 4\frac{3}{7}$

   A. $11\frac{3}{7}$ **B.** $20\frac{2}{7}$

   C. $12\frac{3}{7}$ **D.** $21\frac{2}{7}$

---

34. Subtract $13\frac{7}{15}$ from $22\frac{5}{12}$.

   A. $9\frac{37}{60}$ **B.** $1\frac{19}{20}$

   C. $8\frac{37}{60}$ **D.** $8\frac{19}{20}$

---

35. Find the difference between $36\frac{4}{5}$ and $8\frac{1}{5}$.

   A. $27\frac{3}{4}$ **B.** $27\frac{3}{5}$

   C. $28\frac{3}{5}$ **D.** $28\frac{3}{20}$

---

36. Subtract. $23\frac{1}{6}$

         $-\ 7\frac{3}{4}$

   A. $15\frac{1}{2}$ **B.** $16\frac{7}{12}$

   C. $16\frac{5}{12}$ **D.** $15\frac{5}{12}$

---

37. Subtract 8 from $35\frac{5}{7}$.

   A. $27\frac{5}{7}$ **B.** $26\frac{2}{7}$

   C. 27 **D.** None of these

---

38. Find the difference between 42 and $8\frac{9}{10}$.

   A. $34\frac{9}{10}$ **B.** $34\frac{1}{10}$

   C. $33\frac{9}{10}$ **D.** $33\frac{1}{10}$

Semester Test 1, Form A

Work each problem. Then circle the letter of the best answer.

---

39. $13\frac{3}{5} \times 6\frac{1}{4} = ?$

A. 85 **B.** 80

C. 78 **D.** $\frac{17}{5}$

---

40. $2\frac{5}{14} \times 9\frac{1}{3} = ?$

A. $\frac{11}{2}$ **B.** 22

C. $\frac{44}{6}$ **D.** $\frac{2}{11}$

---

41. $8\frac{1}{6} \times 2\frac{1}{7} = ?$

A. $17\frac{1}{2}$ **B.** 14

C. 16 **D.** None of these

---

42. $4\frac{3}{8} \times 4\frac{2}{7} = ?$

A. $17\frac{1}{7}$ **B.** 5

C. 15 **D.** $18\frac{3}{4}$

---

43. $10\frac{3}{5} \times 1\frac{5}{7} = ?$

A. $19\frac{1}{5}$ **B.** $18\frac{6}{35}$

C. $17\frac{1}{7}$ **D.** $7\frac{4}{7}$

---

44. $4\frac{4}{5} \times 5\frac{2}{3} \times 4\frac{3}{8} = ?$

A. 119 **B.** $\frac{7}{17}$

C. 109 **D.** $\frac{8}{17}$

---

45. $4\frac{1}{2} \div 4\frac{1}{2} = ?$

A. 0 **B.** $20\frac{1}{4}$

C. 11 **D.** 1

---

46. $3\frac{3}{16} \div 4\frac{1}{4} = ?$

A. $\frac{3}{16}$ **B.** $\frac{3}{17}$

C. $\frac{4}{17}$ **D.** $\frac{3}{4}$

Semester Test 1, Form A

Work each problem. Then circle the letter of the best answer.

---

47. $8\frac{1}{10} \div 7\frac{1}{5} = ?$

    A. $\frac{4}{5}$ **B.** $\frac{8}{9}$

    C. $1\frac{1}{4}$ **D.** $1\frac{1}{8}$

---

48. $14\frac{2}{7} \div 3\frac{3}{14} = ?$

    A. $4\frac{4}{9}$ **B.** $\frac{2}{9}$

    C. $2\frac{2}{9}$ **D.** $1\frac{1}{9}$

---

49. $5\frac{10}{13} \div 1\frac{7}{26} = ?$

    A. $2\frac{3}{11}$ **B.** $4\frac{6}{11}$

    C. $\frac{22}{25}$ **D.** $\frac{150}{429}$

---

50. $9\frac{3}{5} \div 3\frac{6}{25} = ?$

    A. $\frac{5}{27}$ **B.** $\frac{16}{27}$

    C. $2\frac{26}{27}$ **D.** $2\frac{80}{81}$

---

51. Write $\frac{5}{8}$ as a decimal.

    A. $1.\overline{6}$ **B.** 0.625

    C. 62.5 **D.** $0.\overline{16}$

---

52. Write $\frac{3}{7}$ as a decimal.

    A. 0.12574 **B.** 0.428571

    C. $0.\overline{12574}$ **D.** $0.\overline{428571}$

---

53. Write 0.84 as a fraction in simplest form.

    A. $\frac{84}{100}$ **B.** $\frac{21}{25}$

    C. $\frac{3}{5}$ **D.** $\frac{12}{30}$

---

54. Write 0.825 as a fraction in simplest form.

    A. $\frac{825}{1,000}$ **B.** $\frac{165}{200}$

    C. $\frac{33}{40}$ **D.** None of these

Semester Test I, Form A

Work each problem. Then circle the letter of the best answer.

---

55. Find the missing value. $\frac{5}{9} = \frac{?}{36}$

A. 20   **B.** 10

C. 40   **D.** None of these

---

56. Find the missing value. $\frac{25}{?} = \frac{5}{13}$

A. 58   **B.** 10

C. 130   **D.** 65

---

57. $7.635 + 0.67 + 8 + 2.4 = ?$

A. 18.605   **B.** 11.505

C. 18.705   **D.** 11.405

---

58. Find the sum of 4.37, 6.2, 36.751, and 500.4.

A. 547.621   **B.** 547.721

C. 546.721   **D.** 647.721

---

59. Add.   5.92
              7.3
              0.601
            $+ \ 0.0047$

A. 13.8267   **B.** 13.8257

C. 12.8257   **D.** 13.8267

---

60. Subtract 6.098 from 8.2036.

A. 2.2056   **B.** 2.8956

C. 1.8956   **D.** 2.1056

---

61. Subtract.   12.7
                  $- \ 8.391$

A. 4.409   **B.** 4.491

C. 4.309   **D.** 5.491

---

62. Subtract 3 from 16.87.

A. 16.84   **B.** 16.57

C. 13.87   **D.** None of these

Basic Computation Series 2000: Quizzes and Tests

Semester Test 1, Form A

Work each problem. Then circle the letter of the best answer.

63. Multiply. $\begin{array}{r} 0.86 \\ \times\ 0.47 \\ \hline \end{array}$	**A.** 0.004042	**B.** 40.42
	C. 4.042	**D.** 0.4042
64. Multiply 16.72 by 7.6.	**A.** 127.072	**B.** 1,270.72
	C. 127.062	**D.** 1,270.62
65. Multiply 0.056 by 0.4.	**A.** 0.0224	**B.** 0.224
	C. 22.4	**D.** 0.0204
66. Divide. $0.67\overline{)542.164}$	**A.** 809.2	**B.** 89.2
	C. 8.92	**D.** 80.92
67. Round 821.649 to the nearest tenth.	**A.** 821.7	**B.** 821.6
	C. 820.0	**D.** 821.65
68. $877.39 \div 100 = ?$	**A.** 87.739	**B.** 87,739
	C. 8.7739	**D.** 8,773.9
69. Divide 7.5808 by 0.92.	**A.** 8.24	**B.** 0.824
	C. 82.4	**D.** 0.0824
70. Divide. $3.6\overline{)2,898}$	**A.** 85	**B.** 805
	C. 8.5	**D.** 80.5

Semester Test 1, Form A

Work each problem. Then circle the letter of the best answer.

---

71. Reduce $\frac{14}{105}$ to lowest terms.

    A. $\frac{14}{105}$ **B.** $\frac{2}{15}$

    C. $\frac{2}{17}$ **D.** $\frac{1}{7}$

---

72. Multiply 36.952 by 100.

    A. 3.6952   **B.** 0.36952

    C. 369.52   **D.** 3,695.2

---

73. List all the divisors of 36.

    A. 1, 2, 3, 6, 9, 12, 18, 36

    B. 2, 3, 4, 6, 9, 12, 18

    C. 1, 2, 3, 4, 6, 9, 12, 18, 36

    D. 1, 2, 3, 4, 6, 8, 9, 12, 18, 36

---

74. Write 24 as the product of prime numbers.

    A. $2 \times 2 \times 6$ **B.** $2 \times 2 \times 2 \times 3$

    C. 2×12 **D.** None of these

---

75. Write in order from smallest to largest: $\frac{1}{2}, \frac{1}{3}, \frac{3}{4}$

    A. $\frac{3}{4}, \frac{1}{3}, \frac{1}{2}$ **B.** $\frac{1}{2}, \frac{1}{3}, \frac{3}{4}$

    C. $\frac{3}{4}, \frac{1}{2}, \frac{1}{3}$ **D.** $\frac{1}{3}, \frac{1}{2}, \frac{3}{4}$

---

76. Find the gross pay for 37 hours at $7.23 per hour.

    A. $267.11   **B.** $276.15

    C. $267.51   **D.** $265.51

---

77. Find the net pay if the gross pay is $157.23 and the deductions are $12.51.

    A. $144.72   **B.** $169.74

    C. $145.32   **D.** $145.72

---

78. Write 17% as a decimal.

    A. 17.00   **B.** 0.17

    C. 1.7   **D.** 0.0017

Semester Test 1, Form A

Work each problem. Then circle the letter of the best answer.

79. Write 42.3% as a decimal.	**A.** 0.423 **C.** 4.23	**B.** 4,230 **D.** 42.30
80. Write 1.67% as a decimal.	**A.** 0.0167 **C.** 16.7	**B.** 1.67 **D.** 167.0
81. Write 0.07 as a percent.	**A.** 70% **C.** 7%	**B.** 0.007% **D.** 700%
82. Write 2.5 as a percent.	**A.** 0.25% **C.** 250%	**B.** 25% **D.** 2.5%
83. Write 0.16 as a percent.	**A.** 1.6% **C.** 160%	**B.** 16% **D.** 0.016%
84. Write $\frac{1}{8}$ as a percent.	**A.** 125% **C.** 8%	**B.** 12.5% **D.** 80%
85. Write $\frac{2}{3}$ as a percent.	**A.** $66\frac{2}{3}$% **C.** 23%	**B.** $33\frac{1}{3}$% **D.** 67%
86. Write $\frac{3}{5}$ as a percent.	**A.** 40% **C.** 35%	**B.** 60% **D.** 350%

Semester Test I, Form A

Work each problem. Then circle the letter of the best answer.

---

87. 15 is what percent of 30?

A. 50%   **B.** $\frac{1}{2}$%

C. 5%   **D.** 200%

---

88. 4 is what percent of 16?

A. 4%   **B.** $\frac{1}{4}$%

C. 25%   **D.** 400%

---

89. 8 is what percent of 12?

A. 23%   **B.** 150%

C. $33\frac{1}{3}$%   **D.** $66\frac{2}{3}$%

---

90. 7 is what percent of 21?

A. $\frac{1}{3}$%   **B.** $33\frac{1}{3}$%

C. 33%   **D.** 3%

---

91. Find 16% of 12.

A. 1.92   **B.** 192

C. 19.2   **D.** 0.192

---

92. What number is 18% of 63?

A. 11.34   **B.** 1.134

C. 113.4   **D.** None of these

---

93. 62% of 47 = ?

A. 29.14   **B.** 2.914

C. 291.4   **D.** 2,914

---

94. Find $33\frac{1}{3}$% of 33.

A. $1\frac{1}{3}$ **B.** 11

C. 3   **D.** 99

Semester Test 1, Form A

Work each problem. Then circle the letter of the best answer.

95. 30 is 12% of what number?	**A.** $2\frac{1}{2}$ **C.** 250	**B.** 3.5 **D.** $\frac{2}{5}$
96. 45 is 90% of what number?	**A.** $\frac{1}{2}$ **C.** 2	**B.** 40.5 **D.** 50
97. 8.71 is 13% of what number?	**A.** 670 **C.** 67	**B.** 1.1323 **D.** 11.323
98. Find the interest on $5,000 at 8% for one year.	**A.** $40,000 **C.** $40	**B.** $400 **D.** $4,000
99. A refrigerator priced at $396 is marked at $132 off the regular price. What is the rate of discount?	**A.** 33% **C.** 50%	**B.** $66\frac{2}{3}\%$ **D.** $33\frac{1}{3}\%$
100. The profit on furniture at the Accent Furniture Store is 25% of the cost to the store. The profit on a table is $75. What did the table cost the store?	**A.** $3,000 **C.** $300	**B.** $18.75 **D.** $187.50

Semester Test 1, Form B

Work each problem. Then circle the letter of the best answer.

1. Add. 726 92 568 9 + 243	**A.** 1,538	**B.** 1,628
	C. 1,638	**D.** 1,528

2. Find the sum of 742 and 9,654.	**A.** 10,396	**B.** 10,406
	C. 9,396	**D.** 10,496

3. Find the total. 3,822 416 5,376 8,026 47 + 7,615	**A.** 24,302	**B.** 25,282
	C. 25,302	**D.** 24,282

4. Add. 6,966 4,321 8,207 + 6,935	**A.** 26,429	**B.** 25,429
	C. 26,419	**D.** 25,419

5. Subtract. 7,652 − 487	**A.** 7,165	**B.** 7,175
	C. 7,164	**D.** 6,165

6. Subtract 2,557 from 7,352.	**A.** 4,805	**B.** 4,795
	C. 4,894	**D.** 4,794

Semester Test I, Form B

Work each problem. Then circle the letter of the best answer.

7. $8,307 - 695 = ?$	**A.** 8,702	**B.** 7,702
	C. 7,612	**D.** 7,712

8. Find the product of 32 and 79.	**A.** 2,528	**B.** 111
	C. 47	**D.** None of these

9. Multiply. $\begin{array}{r} 381 \\ \times\ 905 \\ \hline \end{array}$	**A.** 333,805	**B.** 38,195
	C. 343,805	**D.** 344,805

10. Multiply 509 by 324.	**A.** 19,216	**B.** 19,116
	C. 165,916	**D.** 164,916

11. Divide. $42\overline{)2,730}$	**A.** 605	**B.** 65
	C. 650	**D.** 6,050

12. Divide 36,072 by 9.	**A.** 480	**B.** 408
	C. 48	**D.** 4,008

13. $32,877 \div 9 = ?$	**A.** 36,503	**B.** 36,053
	C. 3,653	**D.** 36,530

14. Add. $\begin{array}{r} \frac{2}{9} \\ +\ \frac{4}{9} \\ \hline \end{array}$	**A.** $\frac{2}{3}$	**B.** $\frac{1}{3}$
	C. $\frac{11}{13}$	**D.** $\frac{8}{9}$

Semester Test 1, Form B

Work each problem. Then circle the letter of the best answer.

---

15. Add $\frac{7}{10}$ and $\frac{7}{15}$.

A. $\frac{7}{30}$ **B.** $1\frac{1}{6}$

C. $\frac{7}{12}$ **D.** $\frac{7}{60}$

---

16. Find the sum of $\frac{5}{8}$ and $\frac{7}{24}$.

A. $\frac{1}{3}$ **B.** $\frac{3}{8}$

C. $\frac{11}{12}$ **D.** $\frac{1}{6}$

---

17. Subtract $\frac{8}{21}$ from $\frac{6}{7}$.

A. $\frac{1}{2}$ **B.** $\frac{26}{21}$

C. $\frac{10}{21}$ **D.** $\frac{2}{5}$

---

18. Subtract $\frac{5}{12}$ from $\frac{4}{5}$.

A. $\frac{73}{60}$ **B.** $\frac{23}{60}$

C. $\frac{27}{60}$ **D.** $\frac{9}{20}$

---

19. $\frac{5}{6} \times \frac{18}{35} = ?$

A. $\frac{3}{7}$ **B.** $\frac{1}{21}$

C. $\frac{90}{210}$ **D.** None of these

---

20. Find the least common denominator for $\frac{9}{35}$ and $\frac{7}{30}$.

A. 120   **B.** 65

C. 5   **D.** 210

---

21. $\frac{3}{4} - \frac{2}{3} = ?$

A. $\frac{1}{12}$ **B.** $\frac{5}{12}$

C. $\frac{1}{4}$ **D.** $\frac{1}{3}$

---

22. $\frac{2}{9} \times \frac{6}{7} = ?$

A. $\frac{1}{2}$ **B.** $\frac{6}{21}$

C. $\frac{3}{7}$ **D.** $\frac{4}{21}$

Semester Test 1, Form B

Work each problem. Then circle the letter of the best answer.

23. $\frac{8}{21} \times \frac{14}{17} \times \frac{13}{20} = ?$	**A.** $\frac{13}{85}$	**B.** $\frac{13}{255}$		
	C. $\frac{52}{51}$	**D.** $\frac{52}{255}$		

24. Divide $\frac{12}{17}$ by 6.	**A.** $4\frac{4}{17}$	**B.** $\frac{2}{17}$	
	C. $\frac{3}{17}$	**D.** $4\frac{16}{17}$	

25. $\frac{2}{5} \div \frac{7}{10} = ?$	**A.** $\frac{7}{25}$	**B.** $\frac{4}{7}$	
	C. $\frac{7}{5}$	**D.** $\frac{7}{4}$	

26. $9 \div \frac{5}{9} = ?$	**A.** $\frac{1}{5}$	**B.** 5	
	C. $16\frac{1}{5}$	**D.** $\frac{5}{81}$	

27. Add. $\quad 19\frac{2}{15}$	**A.** $28\frac{9}{30}$	**B.** $28\frac{3}{5}$	
$\qquad + \; 8\frac{7}{15}$	**C.** $27\frac{9}{30}$	**D.** $27\frac{3}{5}$	

28. Add $14\frac{7}{10}$ and $13\frac{9}{10}$.	**A.** $28\frac{3}{5}$	**B.** $27\frac{3}{5}$	
	C. $27\frac{16}{20}$	**D.** $27\frac{4}{5}$	

29. Find the sum of $12\frac{5}{8}$ and $4\frac{3}{7}$.	**A.** $16\frac{15}{36}$	**B.** $16\frac{8}{15}$	
	C. $17\frac{3}{56}$	**D.** None of these	

30. Add. $\quad 31\frac{3}{4}$	**A.** $40\frac{9}{20}$	**B.** $40\frac{6}{9}$	
$\qquad + \; 9\frac{3}{5}$	**C.** $40\frac{2}{3}$	**D.** $41\frac{7}{20}$	

Semester Test 1, Form B

Work each problem. Then circle the letter of the best answer.

---

31. Find the sum of $18\frac{7}{10}$ and $8\frac{7}{12}$.

    A. $26\frac{49}{120}$ **B.** $26\frac{14}{22}$

    C. $26\frac{7}{11}$ **D.** $27\frac{17}{60}$

---

32. Add. $24\frac{9}{16}$

           $+\ 14\frac{7}{12}$

    A. $38\frac{63}{192}$ **B.** $38\frac{16}{28}$

    C. $38\frac{4}{7}$ **D.** $39\frac{7}{48}$

---

33. Subtract. $12\frac{7}{8}$

           $-\ 7\frac{5}{8}$

    A. $5\frac{1}{8}$ **B.** $5\frac{2}{16}$

    C. $5\frac{1}{4}$ **D.** $4\frac{1}{8}$

---

34. Subtract 14 from $29\frac{3}{5}$.

    A. $14\frac{2}{5}$ **B.** $15\frac{3}{5}$

    C. $15\frac{2}{4}$ **D.** None of these

---

35. Find the difference between $34\frac{2}{3}$ and $7\frac{3}{4}$.

    A. $27\frac{5}{12}$ **B.** $27\frac{11}{12}$

    C. $26\frac{1}{12}$ **D.** $26\frac{11}{12}$

---

36. Subtract. $86\frac{5}{7}$

           $-\ 53\frac{5}{6}$

    A. $32\frac{37}{42}$ **B.** $32\frac{5}{42}$

    C. $33\frac{5}{42}$ **D.** $33\frac{37}{42}$

---

37. Subtract $11\frac{5}{8}$ from 19.

    A. $8\frac{3}{8}$ **B.** $8\frac{5}{8}$

    C. $7\frac{3}{8}$ **D.** $7\frac{5}{8}$

---

38. Find the difference between $27\frac{3}{10}$ and $12\frac{7}{15}$.

    A. $14\frac{5}{6}$ **B.** $15\frac{1}{6}$

    C. $15\frac{5}{30}$ **D.** $15\frac{5}{6}$

Semester Test 1, Form B

Work each problem. Then circle the letter of the best answer.

39. $5\frac{11}{14} \times 3\frac{8}{9} = ?$

A. $22\frac{1}{2}$ **B.** $15\frac{44}{63}$

C. 22 **D.** $8\frac{17}{23}$

40. $3\frac{15}{16} \times 5\frac{1}{7} = ?$

A. $8\frac{16}{23}$ **B.** $15\frac{15}{112}$

C. $20\frac{1}{4}$ **D.** None of these

41. $3\frac{3}{17} \times 7\frac{1}{12} = ?$

A. 27 **B.** $21\frac{1}{68}$

C. $10\frac{4}{29}$ **D.** $22\frac{1}{2}$

42. $4\frac{8}{15} \times 2\frac{5}{8} = ?$

A. $8\frac{1}{3}$ **B.** $11\frac{9}{10}$

C. $6\frac{13}{23}$ **D.** 12

43. $3\frac{15}{26} \times 7\frac{2}{9} = ?$

A. $21\frac{5}{39}$ **B.** $25\frac{5}{6}$

C. 31 **D.** $10\frac{17}{35}$

44. $2\frac{6}{7} \times 2\frac{2}{15} \times 3\frac{1}{16} = ?$

A. $18\frac{2}{3}$ **B.** $12\frac{1}{140}$

C. $7\frac{9}{38}$ **D.** None of these

45. $4\frac{8}{15} \div 6\frac{4}{5} = ?$

A. $2\frac{1}{4}$ **B.** $1\frac{1}{2}$

C. $\frac{4}{9}$ **D.** $\frac{2}{3}$

46. $2\frac{1}{10} \div 1\frac{24}{25} = ?$

A. $\frac{14}{15}$ **B.** $\frac{15}{14}$

C. $\frac{10}{161}$ **D.** $\frac{161}{10}$

Semester Test 1, Form B

Work each problem. Then circle the letter of the best answer.

---

47. $8\frac{1}{10} \div 1\frac{7}{20} = ?$

    A. $8\frac{2}{7}$ **B.** $\frac{1}{6}$

    C. 6 **D.** $11\frac{5}{7}$

---

48. $6\frac{7}{9} \div 6\frac{7}{9} = ?$

    A. 10 **B.** $\frac{61}{81}$

    C. $1\frac{21}{60}$ **D.** 1

---

49. $2\frac{20}{21} \div 4\frac{3}{7} = ?$

    A. $1\frac{1}{2}$ **B.** $\frac{2}{3}$

    C. $\frac{20}{49}$ **D.** $\frac{10}{49}$

---

50. $6\frac{4}{9} \div 9\frac{2}{3} = ?$

    A. $\frac{2}{3}$ **B.** $\frac{3}{2}$

    C. $15\frac{8}{27}$ **D.** $54\frac{8}{27}$

---

51. Write $\frac{7}{12}$ as a decimal.

    A. 0.583 **B.** $0.58\overline{3}$

    C. $0.\overline{583}$ **D.** $0.5\overline{83}$

---

52. Write $\frac{7}{16}$ as a decimal.

    A. $0.437\overline{5}$ **B.** 0.4375

    C. 0.4 **D.** $2.\overline{285714}$

---

53. Write 0.64 as a fraction in simplest form.

    A. $\frac{3}{5}$ **B.** $\frac{64}{100}$

    C. $\frac{16}{25}$ **D.** None of these

---

54. Write 0.128 as a fraction in simplest form.

    A. $\frac{4}{17}$ **B.** $\frac{128}{1,000}$

    C. $\frac{8}{75}$ **D.** $\frac{16}{125}$

Semester Test 1, Form B

Work each problem. Then circle the letter of the best answer.

55. Find the missing value. $\dfrac{3}{17} = \dfrac{39}{?}$	**A.** 42	**B.** 20	
	C. 221	**D.** 56	

56. Find the missing value. $\dfrac{?}{92} = \dfrac{11}{4}$

A. 103   **B.** 253
C. 28   **D.** 96

57. $23.4 + 0.45 + 12 + 6.3 = ?$

A. 27.984   **B.** 42.15
C. 10.434   **D.** 22.314

58. Find the sum of 9.2, 6.75, 400.9 and 63.475.

A. 417.38475   **B.** 83.433
C. 480.325   **D.** None of these

59. Add.
5.96
8.3
0.707
+ 0.0067

A. 14.9737   **B.** 14.9637
C. 13.9737   **D.** 13.9637

60. Subtract 4.709 from 7.0042.

A. 3.7052   **B.** 2.2952
C. 2.3052   **D.** 3.3052

61. Subtract.
14.2
− 7.876

A. 7.476   **B.** 6.476
C. 6.324   **D.** 7.324

62. Subtract 6 from 19.21.

A. 18.41   **B.** 18.61
C. 19.61   **D.** 13.21

Semester Test 1, Form B

Work each problem. Then circle the letter of the best answer.

63. Multiply. $\quad\quad$ 0.92 $\quad\quad\quad\quad$ $\times$ 0.37	**A.** 0.3594 $\quad\quad$ **B.** 0.3394 **C.** 0.3504 $\quad\quad$ **D.** 0.3404
64. Multiply 18.34 by 8.4.	**A.** 144.056 $\quad\quad$ **B.** 154.046 **C.** 154.056 $\quad\quad$ **D.** 144.046
65. Multiply 0.032 by 0.8.	**A.** 2.56 $\quad\quad$ **B.** 0.256 **C.** 0.00256 $\quad\quad$ **D.** 0.0256
66. Divide. $\quad\quad$ 0.82$\overline{)579.494}$	**A.** 76.7 $\quad\quad$ **B.** 706.7 **C.** 7,067 $\quad\quad$ **D.** 70.67
67. $3{,}825.6 \div 100 = ?$	**A.** 38,256 $\quad\quad$ **B.** 3,825,600 **C.** 382.52 $\quad\quad$ **D.** 38.256
68. Divide 5.7685 by 0.83.	**A.** 6.95 $\quad\quad$ **B.** 0.695 **C.** 69.5 $\quad\quad$ **D.** 695
69. Divide 1,666 by 2.8.	**A.** 595 $\quad\quad$ **B.** 59.5 **C.** 5.95 $\quad\quad$ **D.** 59.05
70. Reduce $\frac{20}{120}$ to lowest terms.	**A.** $\frac{1}{5}$ $\quad\quad$ **B.** $\frac{1}{6}$ **C.** $\frac{2}{12}$ $\quad\quad$ **D.** $\frac{4}{24}$

Semester Test 1, Form B

Work each problem. Then circle the letter of the best answer.

---

71. Multiply 8.321 by 1,000.

    A. 83.21   **B.** 832.1

    C. 8,321   **D.** 8.321

---

72. List all the divisors of 40.

    A. 2, 4, 5, 8, 10, 20

    B. 1, 2, 4, 5, 8, 10, 20, 40

    C. 1, 2, 4, 10, 20, 40

    D. 2, 4, 10, 20

---

73. Write 72 as the product of prime numbers.

    A. $2 \times 2 \times 2 \times 3 \times 3$

    B. $2 \times 2 \times 3 \times 3$

    C. $2 \times 2 \times 2 \times 3$

    D. 8×9

---

74. Round 467.537 to the nearest hundredth.

    A. 467.54   **B.** 467.5

    C. 467.540   **D.** 467.53

---

75. Write in order from smallest to largest: $\frac{3}{5}, \frac{5}{8}, \frac{6}{7}$

    A. $\frac{6}{7}, \frac{5}{8}, \frac{3}{5}$ **B.** $\frac{5}{8}, \frac{3}{5}, \frac{6}{7}$

    C. $\frac{3}{5}, \frac{5}{8}, \frac{6}{7}$ **D.** $\frac{6}{7}, \frac{3}{5}, \frac{5}{8}$

---

76. Find the gross pay for 35 hours at $7.25 per hour.

    A. $253.75   **B.** $245.00

    C. $263.20   **D.** None of these

---

77. Find the net pay if the gross pay is $139.62 and the deductions are $14.27.

    A. $153.89   **B.** $125.35

    C. $115.35   **D.** $143.89

---

78. Write 3.5% as a decimal.

    A. 0.35   **B.** 3.5

    C. 350   **D.** 0.035

Semester Test 1, Form B

Work each problem. Then circle the letter of the best answer.

79. Write 53.4% as a decimal.	**A.** 53.4	**B.** 0.534
	C. 0.0534	**D.** 5,340

80. Write 1.82% as a decimal.	**A.** 0.182	**B.** 18.2
	C. 1,820	**D.** 0.0182

81. Write 0.08 as a percent.	**A.** 8%	**B.** 80%
	C. 0.08%	**D.** 0.8%

82. Write 7.2 as a percent.	**A.** 0.072%	**B.** 720%
	C. 72%	**D.** 0.72%

83. Write 0.43 as a percent.	**A.** 43%	**B.** 0.43%
	C. 4.3%	**D.** 430%

84. Write $\frac{3}{4}$ as a percent.	**A.** 125%	**B.** 0.75%
	C. 75%	**D.** 1.25%

85. Write $\frac{2}{9}$ as a percent.	**A.** 0.45%	**B.** 22%
	C. $22\frac{2}{9}$%	**D.** 4.5%

86. Write $\frac{5}{8}$ as a percent.	**A.** 160%	**B.** 0.625%
	C. 16%	**D.** $62\frac{1}{2}$%

Semester Test 1, Form B

Work each problem. Then circle the letter of the best answer.

87. 16 is what percent of 40?	**A.** $\frac{2}{5}$%	**B.** 16%
	C. 40%	**D.** 250%
88. 20 is what percent of 60?	**A.** 20%	**B.** $33\frac{1}{3}$%
	C. $\frac{1}{3}$%	**D.** 300%
89. 15 is what percent of 9?	**A.** $66\frac{2}{3}$%	**B.** 60%
	C. 15%	**D.** $166\frac{2}{3}$%
90. 32 is what percent of 96?	**A.** 300%	**B.** $\frac{1}{3}$%
	C. $33\frac{1}{3}$%	**D.** 32%
91. Find 12% of 63.	**A.** 7.56	**B.** 75.6
	C. 5.25	**D.** 52.5
92. Find 126% of 45.	**A.** 2.8	**B.** 5,670
	C. 0.567	**D.** 56.7
93. Find 6.7% of 43.	**A.** 2.881	**B.** 28.81
	C. 0.02881	**D.** 288.1
94. Find 80% of 75.	**A.** 0.6	**B.** 60
	C. 25	**D.** 93.75

Semester Test 1, Form B

Work each problem. Then circle the letter of the best answer.

95. 162 is 45% of what number?	**A.** 7,290	**B.** 72.9
	C. 3.6	**D.** 360

96. 75 is 150% of what number?	**A.** 50	**B.** 112.5
	C. 11,250	**D.** 500

97. 11.52 is 72% of what number?	**A.** 16	**B.** 8.2944
	C. 0.16	**D.** 829.44

98. Find the interest on $4,850 at 9% for one year.	**A.** $538.88	**B.** $436.50
	C. $4,365.00	**D.** $53.88

99. The regular price of a pair of shoes is $45. From this price, $9 is marked off. What is the rate of discount?	**A.** 40.5%	**B.** 405%
	C. 20%	**D.** 54%

100. An automobile is sale priced at $4,320. This is 90% of the original price. What was the original price?	**A.** $43,200	**B.** $3,888
	C. $4,800	**D.** $5,000

Semester Test 2, Form A

Work each problem. Then circle the letter of the best answer.

1. Measure to the nearest millimeter.

   _____

   A. 2.7 mm   **B.** 4.3 mm

   C. 27 mm   **D.** 43 mm

2. Measure to the nearest tenth-centimeter.

   _____

   A. 5.4 cm   **B.** 54 cm

   C. 0.54 cm   **D.** 540 cm

3. 280 m = ? km

   A. 2,800   **B.** 0.280

   C. 2.8   **D.** 28

4. 47 cm = ? m

   A. 4.7   **B.** 4,700

   C. 0.47   **D.** 0.0047

5. 147 mm = ? cm

   A. 1.47   **B.** 0.147

   C. 14.7   **D.** 1,470

6. 3.83 m = ? mm

   A. 0.383   **B.** 3,830

   C. 38.3   **D.** 383

7. $4\frac{1}{2}$ hours = ? minutes

   A. 270   **B.** 450

   C. $\frac{3}{40}$ **D.** $\frac{5}{6}$

8. 301 days = ? weeks

   A. $75\frac{1}{4}$ **B.** 217

   C. 43   **D.** $12\frac{13}{24}$

Semester Test 2, Form A

Work each problem. Then circle the letter of the best answer.

9.	Add.	3 hr 50 min + 5 hr 55 min	**A.** 9 hr 15 min **B.** 8 hr 15 min **C.** 8 hr 45 min **D.** 9 hr 45 min
10.	Add.	6 mo 3 wk 15 days + 3 mo 3 wk 6 days	**A.** 9 mo 1 wk **B.** 11 mo 1 wk **C.** 10 mo 1 wk **D.** 12 mo 1 wk 3 days
11.	Subtract.	17 hr 32 min − 12 hr 48 min	**A.** 4 hr 12 min **B.** 5 hr 12 min **C.** 5 hr 44 min **D.** 4 hr 44 min
12.	Subtract.	12 yr 3 mo 2 wk − 8 yr 11 mo 5 wk	**A.** 4 yr 8 mo 3 wk **B.** 3 yr 2 mo 7 wk **C.** 4 yr 3 mo 1 wk **D.** 3 yr 3 mo 1 wk
13.	60 °C = ? °F		**A.** 140 **B.** $15\frac{5}{9}$ **C.** 92 **D.** $51\frac{1}{9}$
14.	59 °F = ? °C		**A.** $50\frac{5}{9}$ **B.** 132.2 **C.** 15 **D.** 163.8
15.	Find the measure of ∠A. 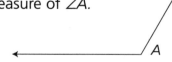		**A.** 60° **B.** 120° **C.** 95° **D.** 165°
16.	Find the measure of ∠B. 		**A.** 35° **B.** 145° **C.** 90° **D.** 175°

Semester Test 2, Form A

Work each problem. Then circle the letter of the best answer.

17. ∠C and ∠D are complementary angles. ∠C measures 47°. Find the measure of ∠D.	**A.** 43°	**B.** 133°	
	C. 137°	**D.** 94°	

18. ∠E and ∠F are complementary angles. ∠E measures 18°. Find the measure of ∠F.	**A.** 108°	**B.** 162°	
	C. 72°	**D.** 136°	

19. ∠G and ∠H are supplementary angles. ∠G measures 25°. Find the measure of ∠H.	**A.** 155°	**B.** 65°	
	C. 115°	**D.** 50°	

20. ∠J and ∠K are supplementary angles. ∠J measures 76°. Find the measure of ∠K.	**A.** 166°	**B.** 14°	
	C. 104°	**D.** 152°	

21. Measure to the nearest quarter-inch.

_____

A. $1\frac{1}{4}$ in.   **B.** $1\frac{3}{4}$ in.

C. $1\frac{1}{2}$ in.   **D.** 1 in.

22. Measure to the nearest quarter-inch.

_____

A. $1\frac{3}{4}$ in.   **B.** 2 in.

C. $1\frac{1}{2}$ in.   **D.** $2\frac{1}{2}$ in.

23. 17 ft = ? yd

A. $5\frac{2}{3}$ **B.** 51

C. $1\frac{5}{12}$ **D.** 204

24. 92 in. = ? ft

A. $130\frac{2}{3}$ **B.** 1,104

C. $7\frac{2}{3}$ **D.** $2\frac{5}{9}$

Semester Test 2, Form A

Work each problem. Then circle the letter of the best answer.

---

25. The length of a paper clip is about _____.

  A. 31 mm   **B.** 31 cm

  C. 31 m   **D.** 31 km

---

26. A jockey has a mass of about _____ kg.

  A. 12   **B.** 100

  C. 3,000   **D.** 45

---

27. Find the area of a rectangle, given $l = 12$ ft and $w = 7$ ft.

  A. 19 ft^2 **B.** 84 ft^2

  C. 36 ft^2 **D.** 42 ft^2

---

28. Find the area of a rectangle, given $l = 21.3$ m and $w = 9.2$ m.

  A. 391.92 m^2 **B.** 30.5 m^2

  C. 195.96 m^2 **D.** 61 m^2

---

29. Find the perimeter of a rectangle, given $l = 25$ cm and $w = 19$ cm.

  A. 10,450 cm   **B.** 44 cm

  C. 20,900 cm   **D.** 88 cm

---

30. Find the perimeter of a rectangle, given $l = 7\frac{1}{2}$ ft and $w = 3\frac{2}{3}$ ft.

  A. $11\frac{1}{6}$ ft   **B.** 165 ft

  C. $27\frac{1}{2}$ ft   **D.** $22\frac{1}{3}$ ft

---

31. The area of a rectangle is 368 ft^2. The width is 16 ft. Find the length.

  A. 5,888 ft   **B.** 168 ft

  C. $11\frac{1}{2}$ ft   **D.** 23 ft

---

32. The area of a rectangle is 49.68 cm^2. The length is 9.2 cm. Find the width.

  A. 15.14 cm   **B.** 447.856 cm

  C. 5.4 cm   **D.** 115.76 cm

Semester Test 2, Form A

Work each problem. Then circle the letter of the best answer.

---

33. The perimeter of a rectangle is 122 mm. The length is 23 mm. Find the width.

A. 38 mm   **B.** 99 mm

C. 145 mm   **D.** 290 mm

---

34. The perimeter of a rectangle is 168 in. The length is 50 in. Find the width.

A. 118 in.   **B.** 84 in.

C. 59 in.   **D.** 34 in.

---

35. Find the area of a triangle, given $b = 21$ ft and $h = 8$ ft.

A. 29 ft^2 **B.** 168 ft^2

C. 84 ft^2 **D.** 13 ft^2

---

36. Find the area of a triangle, given $b = 3.9$ m and $h = 2.4$ m.

A. 9.36 m^2 **B.** 4.68 m^2

C. 6.3 m^2 **D.** 12.6 m^2

---

37. The area of a triangle is 600 yd^2. The base is 75 yd. Find the height.

A. 8 yd   **B.** 16 yd

C. 32 yd   **D.** 675 yd

---

38. The area of a triangle is 32.39 m^2. The height is 7.9 m. Find the base.

A. 4.1 m   **B.** 16.4 m

C. 255.881 m   **D.** 8.2 m

---

39. Find the perimeter of a triangle, given that the sides measure 10 ft, 21 ft, and 17 ft.

A. 43 ft   **B.** 96 ft

C. 24 ft   **D.** 48 ft

---

40. Find the perimeter of a triangle, given that the sides measure 4.0 m, 3.9 m, and 2.5 m.

A. 10.4 m   **B.** 20.8 m

C. 5.2 m   **D.** 19.5 m

Semester Test 2, Form A

Work each problem. Then circle the letter of the best answer.

---

41. Find the area of a parallelogram, given $b = 24$ ft and $h = 11$ ft.

A. 132 ft^2 **B.** 264 ft^2
C. 70 ft^2 **D.** 140 ft^2

---

42. Find the area of a parallelogram, given $b = 7.2$ m and $h = 5$ m.

A. 36 m^2 **B.** 72 m^2
C. 18 m^2 **D.** 24.4 m^2

---

43. Find the perimeter of a parallelogram, given that the measures of two sides are 59 ft and 23 ft.

A. 41 ft **B.** 82 ft
C. 164 ft **D.** 1,357 ft

---

44. Find the perimeter of a parallelogram, given that the measures of two sides are 8.3 m and 7.9 m.

A. 16.2 m **B.** 32.4 m
C. 76.36 m **D.** 8.1 m

---

45. Find the area of a trapezoid, given $b_1 = 7$ in., $b_2 = 13$ in., and $h = 4$ in., where b_1 and b_2 represent the bases.

A. 80 in.^{2} **B.** 40 in.^{2}
C. 364 in.^{2} **D.** 24 in.^{2}

---

46. Find the area of a trapezoid, given $b_1 = 1.3$ m, $b_2 = 3.4$ m, and $h = 0.8$ m, where b_1 and b_2 represent the bases.

A. 0.94 m^2 **B.** 3.76 m^2
C. 1.88 m^2 **D.** 5.5 m^2

---

47. Find the perimeter of a trapezoid, given bases $b_1 = 27$ ft and $b_2 = 83$ ft, and sides with measures 61 ft and 75 ft.

A. 123 ft **B.** 246 ft
C. 492 ft **D.** None of these

---

48. Find the perimeter of a trapezoid, given bases $b_1 = 43$ cm and $b_2 = 64$ cm, and sides with measures 15 cm and 13 cm.

A. 67.5 cm **B.** 270 cm
C. 135 cm **D.** None of these

Semester Test 2, Form A

Work each problem. Then circle the letter of the best answer.

49. Find the volume of a cube, given edge $e = 7$ in.	**A.** 49 in.^{3} **C.** 28 in.^{3}	**B.** 21 in.^{3} **D.** 343 in.^{3}
50. Find the volume of a cube, given edge $e = 10$ cm.	**A.** 100 cm^3 **C.** 40 cm^3	**B.** 1,000 cm^3 **D.** 30 cm^3
51. Find the surface area of a cube, given edge $e = 13$ ft.	**A.** 1,014 ft^2 **C.** 672 ft^2	**B.** 1,352 ft^2 **D.** 312 ft^2
52. Find the surface area of a cube, given edge $e = 7.1$ m.	**A.** 28.4 m^2 **C.** 201.64 m^2	**B.** 302.46 m^2 **D.** 403.28 m^2
53. Find the volume of a rectangular prism, given $l = 4.1$ cm, $w = 3.2$ cm, and $h = 1.5$ cm.	**A.** 17.6 cm^3 **C.** 39.36 cm^3	**B.** 8.8 cm^3 **D.** 19.68 cm^3
54. Find the volume of a rectangular prism, given $l = 8$ ft, $w = 3$ ft, and $h = 7$ ft.	**A.** 84 ft^3 **C.** 168 ft^3	**B.** 18 ft^3 **D.** 336 ft^3
55. Find the surface area of a rectangular prism, given $l = 17$ ft, $w = 8$ ft, and $h = 12$ ft.	**A.** 436 ft^2 **C.** 340 ft^2	**B.** 872 ft^2 **D.** 300 ft^2
56. Find the surface area of a rectangular prism, given $l = 36$ mm, $w = 19$ mm, and $h = 6$ mm.	**A.** 1,014 mm^2 **C.** 61 mm^2	**B.** 900 mm^2 **D.** 2,028 mm^2

Semester Test 2, Form A

Work each problem. Then circle the letter of the best answer.

57. The triangular base of a triangular prism has base $b = 15$ in. and altitude $a = 10$ in. Find the volume, if the height of the prism is 38 in.	**A.** 2,850 in.^{3} **B.** 5,700 in.^{3} **C.** 1,425 in.^{3} **D.** None of these	
58. The triangular base of a triangular prism has base $b = 7$ cm and altitude $a = 4$ cm. Find the volume, if the height of the prism is 9.3 cm.	**A.** 260.4 cm^3 **B.** 130.2 cm^3 **C.** 65.1 cm^3 **D.** 23.3 cm^3	
59. The triangular base of a triangular pyramid has base $b = 17$ in. and altitude $a = 8$ in. Find the volume, if the height of the pyramid is 9 in.	**A.** 408 in.^{3} **B.** 204 in.^{3} **C.** 1,224 in.^{3} **D.** 225 in.^{3}	
60. The triangular base of a triangular pyramid has base $b = 3.5$ cm and altitude $a = 2.4$ cm. Find the volume, if the height of the pyramid is 4.6 cm.	**A.** 19.32 cm^3 **B.** 38,164 cm^3 **C.** 12.88 cm^3 **D.** 6.44 cm^3	
61. Find the circumference of a circle, given $r = 29$ cm. Use 3.14 for π.	**A.** 2,640.74 cm **B.** 91.06 cm **C.** 32.14 cm **D.** 182.12 cm	
62. Find the circumference of a circle, given $d = 14$ ft. Use $\frac{22}{7}$ for π.	**A.** 88 ft **B.** 44 ft **C.** 154 ft **D.** 308 ft	
63. Find the area of a circle, given $r = 3.5$ m. Use 3.14 for π.	**A.** 43.96 m^2 **B.** 21.98 m^2 **C.** 10.99 m^2 **D.** 38.465 m^2	
64. Find the area of a circle, given $d = 42$ in. Use $\frac{22}{7}$ for π.	**A.** 132 in.^{2} **B.** 1,386 in.^{2} **C.** 5,544 in.^{2} **D.** None of these	

Semester Test 2, Form A

Work each problem. Then circle the letter of the best answer.

---

65. Find the volume of a cylinder, given
$r = 9$ cm and $h = 2$ cm. Use 3.14 for π.

   A. 508.68 cm³   **B.** 2,034.72 cm³

   C. 56.62 cm³   **D.** 21.14 cm³

---

66. Find the volume of a cylinder, given
$r = 35$ in. and $h = 10$ in. Use $\frac{22}{7}$ for π.

   A. 15,400 in.³   **B.** 2,200 in.³

   C. 38,500 in.³   **D.** 7,700 in.³

---

67. Find the surface area of a cylinder, given
$r = 12$ cm and $h = 9$ cm. Use 3.14 for π.

   A. 1,582.56 cm²   **B.** 339.12 cm²

   C. 84.36 cm²   **D.** 169.56 cm²

---

68. Find the surface area of a cylinder, given
$r = 7$ in. and $h = 3$ in. Use $\frac{22}{7}$ for π.

   A. 880 in.²   **B.** 1,100 in.²

   C. 440 in.²   **D.** 70 in.²

---

69. Find the volume of a cone, given
$r = 28$ in. and $h = 12$ in. Use $\frac{22}{7}$ for π.

   A. 1,056 in.³   **B.** 9,856 in.³

   C. 29,568 in.³   **D.** 2,464 in.³

---

70. Find the volume of a cone, given
$r = 8$ cm and $h = 15$ cm. Use 3.14 for π.

   A. 125.6 cm³   **B.** 3,014.4 cm³

   C. 1,004.8 cm³   **D.** 376.8 cm³

---

71. Find the volume of a sphere, given
$r = 6$ cm. Use 3.14 for π.

   A. 678.24 cm³   **B.** 904.32 cm³

   C. 150.72 cm³   **D.** 226.08 cm³

---

72. Find the volume of a sphere, given
$r = 3\frac{1}{2}$ in. Use $\frac{22}{7}$ for π.

   A. $179\frac{2}{3}$ in.³   **B.** $269\frac{1}{2}$ in.³

   C. $44\frac{11}{12}$ in.³   **D.** None of these

Semester Test 2, Form A

Work each problem. Then circle the letter of the best answer.

---

73. Complete by following the pattern.

1, 3, 6, 10, __, __, __, __, __, __

    A. 15, 21, 28, 36, 45, 55

    B. 12, 14, 16, 18, 20, 22

    C. 13, 16, 19, 21, 24, 27

    D. None of these

---

74. Complete by following the pattern.

0, 3, 8, 15, __, __, __, __, __, __

    A. 30, 60, 120, 240, 480, 960

    B. 24, 35, 48, 63, 80, 99

    C. 20, 25, 30, 35, 40, 45

    D. None of these

---

75. Complete by following the pattern.

1, 1, 2, 3, 5, __, __, __, __, __, __

    A. 6, 7, 8, 9, 10, 11

    B. 5, 7, 9, 11, 13, 15

    C. 8, 13, 21, 34, 55, 89

    D. None of these

---

76. Find the average of 43, 57, and 92.

    A. 48   **B.** 96

    C. 192   **D.** 64

---

77. Find the average of 132, 341, 627, 243, and 417.

    A. 440   **B.** 176

    C. 880   **D.** 352

---

78. Find the average of 384, 274, 801, and 673.

    A. $266\frac{1}{2}$ **B.** 1,066

    C. 436   **D.** 533

---

79. Find the square root of 841.

    A. 5.099   **B.** 5.385

    C. 26   **D.** 29

---

80. Find the approximate square root of 24.

    A. 615   **B.** 576

    C. 4.899   **D.** 4.583

Semester Test 2, Form A

Work each problem. Then circle the letter of the best answer.

81. What was the total amount spent for gas and electricity for the first six months of the year?

    A. $331   **B.** $362

    C. $352   **D.** $250

82. What was the total amount spent for gas and electricity for the last six months of the year?

    A. $344   **B.** $209

    C. $286   **D.** $310

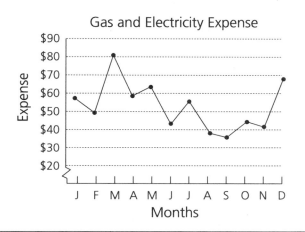

83. What was the total average monthly rainfall for June, July, August, and September?

    A. 22.5 in.   **B.** 19.5 in.

    C. 15.5 in.   **D.** 18 in.

84. What was the total average monthly rainfall for January, February, March, and April?

    A. 17.1 in.   **B.** 25.2 in.

    C. 171 in.   **D.** 8.5 in.

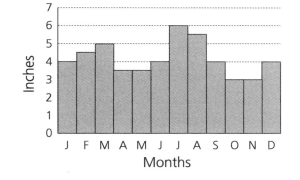

85. If there were 84 points for quizzes, how many points were there for tests?

    A. 231   **B.** 462

    C. 700   **D.** 550

86. If there were 715 points for tests, how many points were there for quizzes?

    A. 400   **B.** 130

    C. 550   **D.** 260

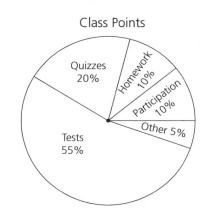

Semester Test 2, Form A

Work each problem. Then circle the letter of the best answer.

---

87. A purchase of $6.72 is taken from $20. What is the most efficient change?

	$10	$5	$1	25¢	10¢	5¢	1¢
A.	1		3		2	1	3
B.	1		3	1			3
C.		1			3		2
D.			13		2	1	3

---

88. A purchase of $11.57 is taken from $20. What is the most efficient change?

	$10	$5	$1	25¢	10¢	5¢	1¢
A.		1	3	1	1	1	3
B.		8		1	1	1	3
C.		1	3		4		3
D.		1	3			8	3

---

89. Which is the best buy?

A. 64 oz for $1.28   **B.** 13 oz for 27¢

C. 20 oz for 46¢   **D.** 32 oz for 61¢

---

90. Which is the best buy?

A. 65 kg for $1.99   **B.** 40 kg for $1.35

C. 124 kg for $4.19   **D.** 354 kg for $11.95

---

91. Anne worked 7 hr 50 min on Monday, 5 hr 20 min on Tuesday, 3 hr 15 min on Wednesday, 6 hr 12 min on Thursday, and 9 hr 35 min on Friday. What was the total time she worked?

A. 31 hr 32 min   **B.** 30 hr 12 min

C. 32 hr 12 min   **D.** 27 hr 19 min

---

92. Find the annual interest earned on $1,500 invested at 13% per year.

A. $115.38   **B.** $19.50

C. $1.95   **D.** $195.00

Semester Test 2, Form A

Work each problem. Then circle the letter of the best answer.

93.	The Lopez family had the following food bills for five months: $276.92, $225.13, $314.16, $205.10, and $245.09. What was the average monthly food cost ?	**A.** $316.60 **C.** $633.20	**B.** $253.28 **D.** $1,266.40
94.	Ricardo drove 3,420 miles on 152 gallons of fuel. How many miles per gallon did he average?	**A.** 15.1 **C.** 22.5	**B.** 19.2 **D.** 30.6
95.	A suit is purchased for $350. The suit is sold at a profit of 17%. Find the selling price.	**A.** $304.50 **C.** $297.50	**B.** $420.00 **D.** $409.50
96.	The Firecracker Express traveled 2,352 miles at an average of 49 miles per hour. How many hours did the trip take?	**A.** 112,896 **C.** 48	**B.** 115,248 **D.** 2,401
97.	Mr. Manycattle earns $15.92 an hour. What is his gross pay for 48 hours of work?	**A.** $76.42 **C.** $764.16	**B.** $7,641.60 **D.** None of these
98.	Leora had a balance of $315.27 in her checking account. She then wrote a check for $28.57. What was her new balance?	**A.** $286.70 **C.** $287.70	**B.** $343.84 **D.** $342.84
99.	A classroom in the shape of a rectangle is 20 ft by 24 ft. How many one-foot square tiles will it take to cover the floor?	**A.** 88 **C.** 960	**B.** 480 **D.** 166
100.	Eric bought a suit for $165.00 at a 40% off sale. What was the original price of the suit?	**A.** $275.00 **C.** $412.50	**B.** $231.00 **D.** $264.00

Semester Test 2, Form B

Work each problem. Then circle the letter of the best answer.

---

1. Measure to the nearest millimeter.

_____

A. 2.3 mm   **B.** 3.2 mm

C. 23 mm   **D.** 32 mm

---

2. Measure to the nearest tenth-centimeter.

_____

A. 0.067 cm   **B.** 67.0 cm

C. 6.7 cm   **D.** 670.0 cm

---

3. 14 km = ? m

A. 1.4   **B.** 14,000

C. 140   **D.** 1,400

---

4. 2.8 m = ? cm

A. 0.028   **B.** 0.28

C. 2,800   **D.** 280

---

5. 142 cm = ? mm

A. 1.42   **B.** 14.2

C. 1,420   **D.** 14,200

---

6. 95 mm = ? m

A. 0.095   **B.** 950

C. 95,000   **D.** 9.5

---

7. 520 min = ? hr

A. $8\frac{2}{3}$ **B.** 31,200

C. $83\frac{2}{3}$ **D.** $\frac{13}{90}$

---

8. 77 weeks = ? days

A. 539   **B.** 11

C. 308   **D.** $19\frac{1}{4}$

Basic Computation Series 2000: Quizzes and Tests

NAME   DATE

Semester Test 2, Form B

Work each problem. Then circle the letter of the best answer.

---

9. Add.

5 hr	48 min
+ 7 hr	55 min

A. 12 hr 43 min **B.** 13 hr 43 min

C. 13 hr 3 min **D.** 12 hr 3 min

---

10. Add.

8 mo	4 wk	27 days
+ 7 mo	9 wk	36 days

A. 20 mo 2 wk **B.** 15 mo 2 wk

C. 18 mo 1 wk **D.** 19 mo 2 wk

---

11. Subtract.

34 hr	15 min
− 18 hr	37 min

A. 15 hr 22 min **B.** 15 hr 38 min

C. 15 hr 78 min **D.** 15 hr 18 min

---

12. Subtract.

17 yr	2 mo	3 wk
− 12 yr	9 mo	5 wk

A. 4 yr 4 mo 2 wk **B.** 16 yr 2 wk

C. 16 yr 2 mo 2 wk **D.** 3 yr 2 mo 2 wk

---

13. 75 °C = ? °F

A. 157 **B.** $23\frac{8}{9}$

C. 167 **D.** 192.6

---

14. 86 °F = ? °C

A. $65\frac{5}{9}$ **B.** $15\frac{5}{9}$

C. $77\frac{7}{9}$ **D.** 30

---

15. Find the measure of ∠A.

A. 43° **B.** 130°

C. 47° **D.** 143°

---

16. Find the measure of ∠B.

A. 64° **B.** 154°

C. 26° **D.** 34°

Copyright © Dale Seymour Publications®

Basic Computation Series 2000: Quizzes and Tests

Semester Test 2, Form B

Work each problem. Then circle the letter of the best answer.

---

17. $\angle C$ and $\angle D$ are complementary angles. $\angle C$ measures 32°. Find the measure of $\angle D$.

A. 122° **B.** 148°
C. 58° **D.** 68°

---

18. $\angle E$ and $\angle F$ are complementary angles. $\angle E$ measures 71°. Find the measure of $\angle F$.

A. 109° **B.** 19°
C. 29° **D.** 42°

---

19. $\angle G$ and $\angle H$ are supplementary angles. $\angle G$ measures 67°. Find the measure of $\angle H$.

A. 23° **B.** 113°
C. 33° **D.** 143°

---

20. $\angle J$ and $\angle K$ are supplementary angles. $\angle J$ measures 42°. Find the measure of $\angle K$.

A. 138° **B.** 58°
C. 48° **D.** 118°

---

21. Measure to the nearest quarter-inch.

_____

A. 2 in. **B.** $2\frac{1}{4}$ in.
C. $2\frac{1}{2}$ in. **D.** $1\frac{3}{4}$ in.

---

22. Measure to the nearest quarter-inch.

_____

A. $\frac{3}{4}$ in. **B.** $\frac{1}{2}$ in.
C. 1 in. **D.** $1\frac{1}{2}$ in.

---

23. 58 yd = ? ft

A. $4\frac{5}{6}$ **B.** $19\frac{1}{3}$
C. 174 **D.** 696

---

24. 47 ft = ? in.

A. 564 **B.** $3\frac{11}{12}$
C. 141 **D.** $15\frac{2}{3}$

Basic Computation Series 2000: Quizzes and Tests

Semester Test 2, Form B

Work each problem. Then circle the letter of the best answer.

25. A man is about _____ tall.	**A.** 2 m **C.** 2 cm	**B.** 2 km **D.** 2 mm
26. A liter of milk has a mass of about _____ g.	**A.** 100 **C.** 10	**B.** 1,000 **D.** 1
27. Find the area of a rectangle, given $l = 14$ ft and $w = 12$ ft.	**A.** 26 ft² **C.** 52 ft²	**B.** 84 ft² **D.** 168 ft²
28. Find the area of a rectangle, given $l = 47.2$ cm and $w = 21.2$ cm.	**A.** 500.32 cm² **C.** 1,000.64 cm²	**B.** 68.4 cm² **D.** 136.8 cm²
29. Find the perimeter of a rectangle, given $l = 14$ m and $w = 9$ m.	**A.** 23 m **C.** 46 m	**B.** 126 m **D.** 63 m
30. Find the perimeter of a rectangle, given $l = 9\frac{2}{3}$ ft and $w = 5\frac{1}{4}$ ft.	**A.** $24\frac{7}{12}$ ft **C.** $14\frac{11}{12}$ ft	**B.** $101\frac{1}{2}$ ft **D.** $29\frac{5}{6}$ ft
31. The area of a rectangle is 714 ft². The width is 17 ft. Find the length.	**A.** 42 ft **C.** 697 ft	**B.** 340 ft **D.** 680 ft
32. The area of a rectangle is 156.18 cm². The length is 13.7 cm. Find the width.	**A.** 142.48 cm **C.** 64.39 cm	**B.** 11.4 cm **D.** 128.78 cm

Semester Test 2, Form B

Work each problem. Then circle the letter of the best answer.

33. The perimeter of a rectangle is 156 cm. The length is 48 cm. Find the width.	**A.** 7,488 cm	**B.** 30 cm	
	C. 3.25 cm	**D.** 108 cm	

34. The perimeter of a rectangle is 204 ft The length is 62 ft. Find the width.	**A.** 40 ft	**B.** 71 ft	
	C. 142 ft	**D.** 12,648 ft	

35. Find the area of a triangle, given $b = 35$ ft and $h = 20$ ft.	**A.** 700 ft^2	**B.** 350 ft^2	
	C. 110 ft^2	**D.** 55 ft^2	

36. Find the area of a triangle, given $b = 8.2$ m and $h = 12.4$ m.	**A.** 101.68 m^2	**B.** 25.42 m^2	
	C. 50.84 m^2	**D.** 41.2 m^2	

37. The area of a triangle is 189 ft^2. The base is 27 ft. Find the height.	**A.** 28 ft	**B.** 7 ft	
	C. 14 ft	**D.** 162 ft	

38. The area of a triangle is 586.16 cm^2. The height is 27.2 cm. Find the base.	**A.** 86.2 cm	**B.** 21.55 cm	
	C. 43.1 cm	**D.** 265.88 cm	

39. Find the perimeter of a triangle, given that the sides measure 27 in., 36 in., and 46 in.	**A.** 109 in.	**B.** $54\frac{1}{2}$ in.	
	C. 218 in.	**D.** 136 in.	

40. Find the perimeter of a triangle, given that the sides measure 72 cm, 81 cm, and 97 cm.	**A.** 250 cm	**B.** 125 cm	
	C. 500 cm	**D.** 322 cm	

Semester Test 2, Form B

Work each problem. Then circle the letter of the best answer.

41. Find the area of a parallelogram, given $b = 7.5$ m and $h = 3.7$ m.	**A.** 22.4 m^2 **C.** 13.87 m^2	**B.** 55.5 m^2 **D.** 27.75 m^2	
42. Find the area of a parallelogram, given $b = 63$ in. and $h = 24$ in.	**A.** 174 in.^{2} **C.** 756 in.^{2}	**B.** 378 in.^{2} **D.** 1,512 in.^{2}	
43. Find the perimeter of a parallelogram, given that the measures of two sides are 62 cm and 94 cm.	**A.** 2,914 cm **C.** 156 cm	**B.** 5,828 cm **D.** 312 cm	
44. Find the perimeter of a parallelogram, given that the measures of two sides are 12.6 m and 15.9 m.	**A.** 114 m **C.** 28.5 m	**B.** 57 m **D.** 14.25 m	
45. Find the area of a trapezoid, given $b_1 = 12$ m, $b_2 = 7$ m, and $h = 6$ m, where b_1 and b_2 represent the bases.	**A.** 25 m^2 **C.** 66 m^2	**B.** 114 m^2 **D.** 57 m^2	
46. Find the area of a trapezoid, given $b_1 = 36$ in., $b_2 = 48$ in., and $h = 21$ in., where b_1 and b_2 represent the bases.	**A.** 1,764 in.^{2} **C.** 441 in.^{2}	**B.** 882 in.^{2} **D.** 1,044 in.^{2}	
47. Find the perimeter of a trapezoid, given bases $b_1 = 32$ yd and $b_2 = 29$ yd, and sides with measures 24 yd and 17 yd.	**A.** 469 yd **C.** 51 yd	**B.** 204 yd **D.** 102 yd	
48. Find the perimeter of a trapezoid, given bases $b_1 = 48$ cm and $b_2 = 81$ cm, and sides with measures 63 cm and 51 cm.	**A.** 486 cm **C.** 121.5 cm	**B.** 243 cm **D.** 3,342 cm	

Semester Test 2, Form B

Work each problem. Then circle the letter of the best answer.

---

49. Find the volume of a cube, given edge $e = 5$ cm.

A. 30 cm³   **B.** 15 cm³
C. 125 cm³   **D.** 20 cm³

---

50. Find the volume of a cube, given edge $e = 14$ in.

A. 2,744 in.³   **B.** 56 in.³
C. 84 in.³   **D.** 42 in.³

---

51. Find the surface area of a cube, given edge $e = 25$ ft.

A. 100 ft²   **B.** 2,500 ft²
C. 150 ft²   **D.** 3,750 ft²

---

52. Find the surface area of a cube, given edge $e = 12.2$ cm.

A. 595.36 cm²   **B.** 148.84 cm²
C. 73.2 cm²   **D.** 893.04 cm²

---

53. Find the volume of a rectangular prism, given $l = 8\frac{1}{2}$ ft, $w = 4$ ft, and $h = 2\frac{1}{4}$ ft.

A. $76\frac{1}{2}$ ft³   **B.** 153 ft³
C. $14\frac{3}{4}$ ft³   **D.** $71\frac{1}{2}$ ft³

---

54. Find the volume of a rectangular prism, given $l = 7.3$ m, $w = 8.1$ m, and $h = 5.7$ m.

A. 674.082 m³   **B.** 337.041 m³
C. 53.47 m³   **D.** 42.2 m³

---

55. Find the surface area of a rectangular prism, given $l = 24$ ft, $w = 17$ ft, and $h = 12$ ft.

A. 900 ft²   **B.** 492 ft²
C. 1,800 ft²   **D.** 612 ft²

---

56. Find the surface area of a rectangular prism, given $l = 25$ cm, $w = 19$ cm, and $h = 13$ cm.

A. 1,522 cm²   **B.** 1,275 cm²
C. 1,047 cm²   **D.** 2,094 cm²

Semester Test 2, Form B

Work each problem. Then circle the letter of the best answer.

57. The triangular base of a triangular prism has base $b = 25$ in. and altitude $a = 13$ in. Find the volume, if the height of the prism is 22 in.	**A.** 7,150 in.^{3} **C.** 3,575 in.^{3}	**B.** 836 in.^{3} **D.** $1,191\frac{2}{3}$ in.^{3}
58. The triangular base of a triangular prism has base $b = 2.3$ cm and altitude $a = 3.1$ cm. Find the volume, if the height of the prism is 1.4 cm.	**A.** 9.982 cm^3 **C.** 7.56 cm^3	**B.** 4.991 cm^3 **D.** 1.66 cm^3
59. The triangular base of a triangular pyramid has base $b = 27$ in. and altitude $a = 12$ in. Find the volume, if the height of the pyramid is 13 in.	**A.** 702 in.^{3} **C.** 6,318 in.^{3}	**B.** 2,106 in.^{3} **D.** 4,212 in.^{3}
60. The triangular base of a triangular pyramid has base $b = 18$ cm and altitude $a = 11$ cm. Find the volume, if the height of the pyramid is 5.1 cm.	**A.** 504.9 cm^3 **C.** 336.6 cm^3	**B.** 1,009.1 cm^3 **D.** 168.3 cm^3
61. Find the circumference of a circle, given $r = 15$ cm. Use 3.14 for π.	**A.** 94.2 cm **C.** 47.1 cm	**B.** 706.5 cm **D.** 1,413 cm
62. Find the circumference of a circle, given $d = 21$ ft. Use $\frac{22}{7}$ for π.	**A.** 66 ft **C.** 33 ft	**B.** 1,386 ft **D.** 346.5 ft
63. Find the area of a circle, given $r = 3\frac{1}{2}$ ft. Use $\frac{22}{7}$ for π.	**A.** $19\frac{1}{4}$ ft^2 **C.** 308 ft^2	**B.** 154 ft^2 **D.** $38\frac{1}{2}$ ft^2
64. Find the area of a circle, given $r = 2.5$ m. Use 3.14 for π.	**A.** 19.625 m^2 **C.** 625 m^2	**B.** 7.85 m^2 **D.** 15.7 m^2

Semester Test 2, Form B

Work each problem. Then circle the letter of the best answer.

65. Find the volume of a cylinder, given $r = 8$ cm and $h = 5$ cm. Use 3.14 for π.	**A.** 125.6 cm³ **B.** 1,004.8 cm³ **C.** 630 cm³ **D.** 502.4 cm³
66. Find the volume of a cylinder, given $r = 28$ in. and $h = 10$ in. Use $\frac{22}{7}$ for π.	**A.** 12,320 in.³ **B.** 2,464 in.³ **C.** 24,640 in.³ **D.** 880 in.³
67. Find the surface area of a cylinder, given $r = 9.5$ cm and $h = 6$ cm. Use 3.14 for π.	**A.** 357.96 cm² **B.** 178.98 cm² **C.** 1,700.31 cm² **D.** 924.73 cm²
68. Find the surface area of a cylinder, given $r = 16$ in. and $h = 19$ in. Use $\frac{22}{7}$ for π.	**A.** 28,160 in.² **B.** 1,760 in.² **C.** 3,520 in.² **D.** 14,030 in.²
69. Find the volume of a cone, given $r = 12$ in. and $h = 14$ in. Use $\frac{22}{7}$ for π.	**A.** 6,336 in.³ **B.** 2,112 in.³ **C.** 1,006 in.³ **D.** 2,464 in.³
70. Find the volume of a cone, given $r = 15$ cm and $h = 13$ cm. Use 3.14 for π.	**A.** 2,653.3 cm³ **B.** 9,184.5 cm³ **C.** 3,061.5 cm³ **D.** 204.1 cm³
71. Find the volume of a sphere, given $r = 3$ m. Use 3.14 for π.	**A.** 339.12 m³ **B.** 113.04 m³ **C.** 37.68 m³ **D.** 84.78 m³
72. Find the volume of a sphere, given $r = 9$ ft. Use 3.14 for π.	**A.** 9,156.24 ft³ **B.** 28.26 ft³ **C.** 3,052.08 ft³ **D.** 254.34 ft³

Semester Test 2, Form B

Work each problem. Then circle the letter of the best answer.

---

73. Complete by following the pattern.

5, 6, 10, 19, __, __, __, __, __, __

  A. 28, 37, 46, 55, 64, 73

  B. 35, 60, 96, 145, 209, 290

  C. 11, 12, 13, 14, 15, 16

  D. None of these

---

74. Complete by following the pattern.

2, 5, 10, 17, __, __, __, __, __, __

  A. 22, 27, 32, 37, 42, 47

  B. 24, 31, 38, 45, 52, 59

  C. 26, 37, 50, 65, 82, 101

  D. None of these

---

75. Complete by following the pattern.

3, 9, 19, 33, __, __, __, __, __, __

  A. 51, 73, 99, 129, 163, 201

  B. 43, 53, 63, 73, 83, 93

  C. 47, 61, 75, 89, 103, 127

  D. None of these

---

76. Find the average of 63, 72, and 96.

  A. 462   **B.** 231

  C. $115\frac{1}{2}$ **D.** 77

---

77. Find the average of 164, 341, 265, 506, and 234.

  A. 755   **B.** 302

  C. 151   **D.** 1,510

---

78. Find the average of 523, 635, 432, and 714.

  A. 2,304   **B.** 1,152

  C. 288   **D.** 576

---

79. Find the square root of 1,369.

  A. 6.164   **B.** 6.083

  C. 43   **D.** 37

---

80. Find the approximate square root of 51.

  A. 2,601   **B.** 7.681

  C. 7.141   **D.** 3,481

Semester Test 2, Form B

Work each problem. Then circle the letter of the best answer.

81. Which country has the greatest difference between birth rate and death rate?

    A. Mexico   **B.** United Kingdom

    C. France   **D.** India

82. Which country has the least difference between birth rate and death rate?

    A. Mexico   **B.** United Kingdom

    C. France   **D.** India

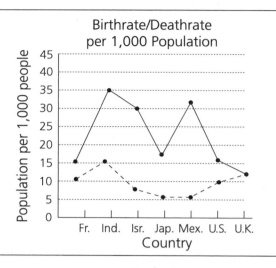

Birthrate/Deathrate per 1,000 Population

83. If the budget is $3,400, how much is spent on food?

    A. $578   **B.** $170

    C. $57,800   **D.** $1,700

84. If the budget is $3,900, how much is spent on shelter and utilities?

    A. $858   **B.** $1,950

    C. $4,368   **D.** $1,209

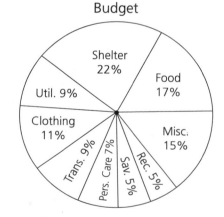

Budget

85. Which city has a population between 3 and 4 million?

    A. New York   **B.** Los Angeles

    C. Chicago   **D.** Houston

86. Which city has a population between 2 and 3 million?

    A. Chicago   **B.** New York

    C. Los Angeles   **D.** Houston

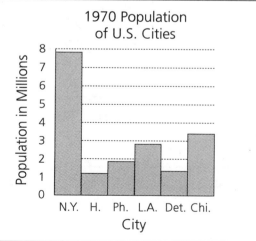

1970 Population of U.S. Cities

Semester Test 2, Form B

Work each problem. Then circle the letter of the best answer.

---

87. A purchase of $7.81 is taken from $20. What is the most efficient change?

	$10	$5	$1	25¢	10¢	5¢	1¢
A.	1		2		3		1
B.			12			3	4
C.	1		2	3		1	1
D.	1		2		1	1	4

---

88. A purchase of $13.87 is taken from $20. What is the most efficient change?

	$10	$5	$1	25¢	10¢	5¢	1¢
A.		1	1			2	3
B.		1	1		1		3
C.	1		3	3	1		2
D.	1		3		8		2

---

89. Which is the best buy?

    A. 102 oz for $3.25 **B.** 16 oz for $0.56

    C. 64 oz for $2.05 **D.** 32 oz for $0.99

---

90. Which is the best buy?

    A. 325 kg for $8.12 **B.** 200 kg for $5.40

    C. 250 kg for $7.75 **D.** 400 kg for $10.80

---

91. Leah worked 5 hr 20 min on Monday, 7 hr 55 min on Tuesday, 3 hr 27 min on Wednesday, 8 hr 43 min on Thursday, and 7 hr 45 min on Friday. What was the total time she worked?

    A. 33 hr 10 min   **B.** 30 hr 10 min

    C. 30 hr   **D.** 33 hr

---

92. Find the annual interest earned on $1,750 invested at 12% per year.

    A. $105   **B.** $21,000

    C. $21   **D.** $210

Semester Test 2, Form B

Work each problem. Then circle the letter of the best answer.

---

93. Juanita made grades of 95, 84, 73, 87, 79, and 92 on six tests. What was her average grade?

   A. 87   **B.** 85

   C. 73   **D.** 83

---

94. Hamilton took 19 hours to drive 741 miles. What was his average rate for the trip?

   A. 14,079 mph   **B.** 39 mph

   C. 57 mph   **D.** None of these

---

95. A dress marked $49.50 is on sale for 30% off. What is the sale price?

   A. $84.15   **B.** $14.85

   C. $64.35   **D.** $34.65

---

96. A dealer sold 5 new cars for a total of $180,725. What was the average price of the cars he sold?

   A. $36,000   **B.** $903,625

   C. $36,145   **D.** $360,145

---

97. Kevin earns $7.50 an hour. What is his net pay if he works 38 hours and has deductions totaling $8.15?

   A. $276.85   **B.** $285

   C. $293.15   **D.** $594.70

---

98. A room measure 27 feet by 45 feet. How many square yards of carpet are required to cover the floor?

   A. 45   **B.** 162

   C. 81   **D.** 135

---

99. Helen had a balance of $324.42 in her checking account. She deposited checks of $39.51, $48.72, and $112.19. What was her balance after the deposits?

   A. $124.00   **B.** $200.42

   C. $524.84   **D.** None of these

---

100. A total of 702 students purchased the yearbook. This was 78% of the school enrollment. What was the enrollment?

   A. 900   **B.** 1,200

   C. 1,000   **D.** None of these

         Basic Computation Series 2000: Quizzes and Tests

Answers to Exercises

PAGE 1
1. 31 **2.** 451,841 **3.** 792 **4.** 1,043 **5.** 200 **6.** 159 **7.** 1,290
8. 1,435 **9.** 7,019,491 **10.** 12,505 **11.** 28,813 **12.** 53,605,943
13. 407,697 **14.** 293,672 **15.** 891

PAGE 2
1. 31 **2.** 684,382 **3.** 925 **4.** 1,115 **5.** 260 **6.** 146 **7.** 1,223
8. 1,645 **9.** 717,040 **10.** 13,581 **11.** 38,826 **12.** 50,712,022
13. 507,507 **14.** 380,034 **15.** 1,005

PAGE 3
1. 32 **2.** 633,801 **3.** 819 **4.** 608 **5.** 335 **6.** 201 **7.** 1,776
8. 1,417 **9.** 825,882 **10.** 11,449 **11.** 44,637 **12.** 78,645,522
13. 807,974 **14.** 675,414 **15.** 1,228

PAGE 4
1. 30 **2.** 443,535 **3.** 894 **4.** 982 **5.** 215 **6.** 159 **7.** 2,063
8. 1,585 **9.** 8,022,935 **10.** 14,777 **11.** 60,441 **12.** 68,519,514
13. 907,369 **14.** 441,398 **15.** 1,335

PAGE 5
1. 374 **2.** 401 **3.** 69,407 **4.** 5,125 **5.** 7,959 **6.** 642 **7.** 559
8. 439 **9.** 212 **10.** 3,394 **11.** 46,177 **12.** 715,692 **13.** 3,565
14. 426 **15.** 702,625

PAGE 6
1. 322 **2.** 174 **3.** 46,258 **4.** 589 **5.** 36,682 **6.** 34 **7.** 67 **8.** 199
9. 278 **10.** 69,072 **11.** 83,953 **12.** 454,849 **13.** 304 **14.** 1,962
15. 539,432

PAGE 7
1. 81,171 **2.** 1,110 **3.** 6,038 **4.** 15,142 **5.** 15,969 **6.** 473
7. 8,859 **8.** 65,821 **9.** 1,909 **10.** 5,556 **11.** 5,521 **12.** 8,788
13. 51 **14.** 5,889 **15.** 46,779

PAGE 8
1. 60,919 **2.** 9,005 **3.** 65,813 **4.** 25,883 **5.** 17,877 **6.** 499
7. 21,819 **8.** 5,244 **9.** 2,907 **10.** 23,587 **11.** 22,096 **12.** 29,091
13. 201 **14.** 17,509 **15.** 56,068

PAGE 9
1. 27 **2.** 392 **3.** 345 **4.** 140 **5.** 324 **6.** 280 **7.** 105 **8.** 603
9. 371 **10.** 7,740 **11.** 5,139 **12.** 816

PAGE 10
1. 102 **2.** 160 **3.** 29 **4.** 324 **5.** 294 **6.** 180 **7.** 80 **8.** 243
9. 294 **10.** 1,377 **11.** 2,136 **12.** 2,436

PAGE 11
1. 45 **2.** 120 **3.** 108 **4.** 252 **5.** 376 **6.** 261 **7.** 2,217 **8.** 5,283
9. 828 **10.** 2,985 **11.** 5,901 **12.** 11,488

PAGE 12
1. 84 **2.** 2,736 **3.** 3,132 **4.** 1,788 **5.** 4,215 **6.** 8,376 **7.** 696
8. 4,617 **9.** 4,192 **10.** 2,034 **11.** 1,612 **12.** 589

PAGE 13
1. 180 **2.** 840 **3.** 160 **4.** 3,948 **5.** 1,470 **6.** 3,916 **7.** 1,290
8. 6,739 **9.** 26,934 **10.** 12,420 **11.** 27,945 **12.** 75,072

PAGE 14
1. 595 **2.** 720 **3.** 2,204 **4.** 3,108 **5.** 320 **6.** 1,829 **7.** 17,556
8. 4,108 **9.** 12,410 **10.** 21,567 **11.** 26,880 **12.** 42,164

PAGE 15
1. 1,075 **2.** 1,120 **3.** 2,314 **4.** 741 **5.** 4,368 **6.** 520 **7.** 9,108
8. 32,712 **9.** 5,662 **10.** 18,688 **11.** 39,886 **12.** 4,410

PAGE 16
1. 940 **2.** 468 **3.** 900 **4.** 884 **5.** 6,975 **6.** 1,230 **7.** 33,990
8. 37,656 **9.** 68,262 **10.** 15,360 **11.** 21,112 **12.** 26,625

PAGE 17
1. 24,345 **2.** 3,572 **3.** 256,690 **4.** 2,106 **5.** 74,601 **6.** 2,044
7. 1,776 **8.** 12,193 **9.** 0 **10.** 684 **11.** 841,960 **12.** 391

PAGE 18
1. 93,852 **2.** 4,464 **3.** 4,059,594 **4.** 1,836 **5.** 76,912 **6.** 3,293
7. 4,752 **8.** 1,094,457 **9.** 1,083 **10.** 375 **11.** 1,564 **12.** 168

PAGE 19
1. 59,056 **2.** 2,241 **3.** 263,835 **4.** 2,331 **5.** 83,842 **6.** 1,918
7. 4,515 **8.** 9,116 **9.** 0 **10.** 385 **11.** 3,195,360 **12.** 384

PAGE 20
1. 55,376 **2.** 546 **3.** 375,669 **4.** 2,183 **5.** 421,902 **6.** 4,232
7. 1,428 **8.** 101,565 **9.** 0 **10.** 3,416 **11.** 2,519,850 **12.** 756

PAGE 21
1. 9 **2.** 6 **3.** 7 **4.** 0 **5.** 8 **6.** 8 **7.** 9 **8.** 8 **9.** 7 **10.** 5 **11.** 3
12. 7 **13.** 10 **14.** 8 **15.** 9 **16.** 5 **17.** 4 **18.** 5 **19.** 3 **20.** 6
21. 10 **22.** 4 **23.** 6 **24.** 4 **25.** 8 **26.** 6 **27.** 7 **28.** 5 **29.** 0 **30.** 2

PAGE 22
1. 8 r 2 **2.** 8 r 1 **3.** 7 r 1 **4.** 8 r 2 **5.** 5 r 1 **6.** 7 r 3 **7.** 5 r 3
8. 6 r 2 **9.** 4 r 1 **10.** 6 r 6 **11.** 6 r 2 **12.** 6 r 3 **13.** 4 r 7
14. 6 r 3 **15.** 6 r 1 **16.** 8 r 2 **17.** 9 r 2 **18.** 9 r 2 **19.** 7 r 5
20. 7 r 5 **21.** 5 r 2 **22.** 8 r 3 **23.** 4 r 3 **24.** 6 r 5 **25.** 10 r 1
26. 8 r 1 **27.** 6 r 1 **28.** 3 r 3 **29.** 8 r 3 **30.** 9 r 1

PAGE 23
1. 3 r 1 **2.** 2 r 2 **3.** 7 r 1 **4.** 6 r 3 **5.** 7 r 1 **6.** 4 r 4 **7.** 6 r 1
8. 5 r 4 **9.** 6 r 3 **10.** 7 r 3 **11.** 4 r 4 **12.** 7 r 3 **13.** 7 r 2
14. 6 r 7 **15.** 9 r 1 **16.** 4 r 6 **17.** 3 r 2 **18.** 5 r 1 **19.** 8 r 5
20. 7 r 2 **21.** 4 r 3 **22.** 6 r 6 **23.** 3 r 5 **24.** 2 r 3 **25.** 8 r 1
26. 14 r 3 **27.** 8 r 1 **28.** 7 r 1 **29.** 3 r 2 **30.** 9 r 2

PAGE 24
1. 9 r 3 **2.** 6 r 6 **3.** 11 r 1 **4.** 5 r 6 **5.** 5 r 2 **6.** 3 r 1 **7.** 3 r 6
8. 5 r 4 **9.** 5 r 7 **10.** 3 r 4 **11.** 4 r 7 **12.** 7 r 3 **13.** 6 r 1
14. 11 r 2 **15.** 5 r 1 **16.** 3 r 1 **17.** 2 r 4 **18.** 6 r 2 **19.** 4 r 1
20. 2 r 6 **21.** 5 r 1 **22.** 3 r 2 **23.** 5 r 2 **24.** 3 r 1 **25.** 7 r 3
26. 4 r 2 **27.** 5 r 5 **28.** 14 r 2 **29.** 7 r 4 **30.** 5 r 2

PAGE 25
1. 42 **2.** 19 **3.** 92 **4.** 27 **5.** 61 **6.** 89 **7.** 67 **8.** 91 **9.** 67
10. 88 **11.** 31 **12.** 87

PAGE 26

1. 77 **2.** 89 **3.** 23 **4.** 46 **5.** 52 **6.** 71 **7.** 37 **8.** 68 **9.** 27 **10.** 50 **11.** 83 **12.** 49

PAGE 27

1. 67 **2.** 23 **3.** 47 **4.** 36 **5.** 71 **6.** 29 **7.** 79 **8.** 52 **9.** 29 **10.** 57 **11.** 63 **12.** 42

PAGE 28

1. 79 **2.** 81 **3.** 46 **4.** 36 **5.** 24 **6.** 83 **7.** 42 **8.** 95 **9.** 37 **10.** 56 **11.** 63 **12.** 25

PAGE 29

1. 29 **2.** 36 **3.** 72 **4.** 59 **5.** 67 **6.** 43 **7.** 26 **8.** 17 **9.** 58 **10.** 35 **11.** 78 **12.** 67

PAGE 30

1. 23 **2.** 17 **3.** 32 **4.** 41 **5.** 92 **6.** 47 **7.** 32 **8.** 58 **9.** 45 **10.** 52 **11.** 41 **12.** 27

PAGE 31

1. 21 **2.** 48 **3.** 22 **4.** 41 **5.** 32 **6.** 15 **7.** 26 **8.** 52 **9.** 14 **10.** 62 **11.** 27 **12.** 32

PAGE 32

1. 43 **2.** 51 **3.** 49 **4.** 22 **5.** 47 **6.** 33 **7.** 51 **8.** 44 **9.** 32 **10.** 43 **11.** 16 **12.** 21

PAGE 33

1. 61 **2.** 154 **3.** 4 **4.** 48 **5.** 131 **6.** 8 **7.** 70 **8.** 347 **9.** 300 **10.** 7 **11.** 24 **12.** 704

PAGE 34

1. 99 **2.** 21 **3.** 81,039 **4.** 2 **5.** 23 **6.** 6 **7.** 24 **8.** 63 **9.** 100 **10.** 17 **11.** 13 **12.** 321

PAGE 35

1. 53 **2.** 169 **3.** 178 **4.** 252 **5.** 26,129 **6.** 10 **7.** 41 **8.** 25 **9.** 252 **10.** 31 **11.** 47 **12.** 4,003

PAGE 36

1. 23 **2.** 451 **3.** 219 **4.** 65 **5.** 352 **6.** 34 **7.** 546 **8.** 69 **9.** 10,101 **10.** 3 **11.** 512 **12.** 46

PAGE 37

1. 297 **2.** 1,171,275 **3.** 2,598 **4.** 417,978 **5.** 136,889 **6.** 128,149 **7.** 2,436 **8.** 220,125 **9.** 452,501 **10.** 613 **11.** 564 **12.** 3,005

PAGE 38

1. 273 **2.** 1,218,829 **3.** 2,116 **4.** 757,878 **5.** 289,889 **6.** 207,979 **7.** 3,216 **8.** 333,795 **9.** 284,214 **10.** 909 **11.** 217 **12.** 9,044

PAGE 39

1. 239 **2.** 1,657,395 **3.** 2,014 **4.** 728,174 **5.** 18,888 **6.** 648,567 **7.** 1,276 **8.** 222,396 **9.** 565,410 **10.** 81 **11.** 414 **12.** 3,005

PAGE 40

1. 273 **2.** 1,072,583 **3.** 2,965 **4.** 609,707 **5.** 517,729 **6.** 441,988 **7.** 3,886 **8.** 127,576 **9.** 63,756 **10.** 705 **11.** 317 **12.** 4,006

PAGE 41

1. 5,506 **2.** 1,119 **3.** 378 **4.** 6,048 **5.** $2,875 **6.** 8 **7.** $5,985 **8.** $4

PAGE 42

1. 472,410 **2.** $648 **3.** 5,895 m **4.** $1,801 **5.** $1,800 **6.** 4,464 **7.** 16 **8.** 45

PAGE 43

1. 2,363 **2.** $1,868 **3.** 68,782 **4.** 645 **5.** $405 **6.** 39,215 **7.** 38 **8.** $816

PAGE 44

1. 617 **2.** 1,281,247 mi^2 **3.** 10,705 ft **4.** $67,875 **5.** 7,680 **6.** 20,805 **7.** $22 **8.** 98

PAGE 45

1. = **2.** ≠ **3.** ≠ **4.** 80 **5.** 1 **6.** 21 **7.** 44 **8.** 78 **9.** 152 **10.** 184 **11.** 35 **12.** 171

PAGE 46

1. ≠ **2.** ≠ **3.** = **4.** 20 **5.** 4 **6.** 7 **7.** 9 **8.** 7 **9.** 3 **10.** 11 **11.** 5 **12.** 12

PAGE 47

1. ≠ **2.** = **3.** = **4.** 12 **5.** 24 **6.** 100 **7.** 33 **8.** 12 **9.** 4 **10.** 6 **11.** 9 **12.** 6

PAGE 48

1. ≠ **2.** ≠ **3.** = **4.** 80 **5.** 7 **6.** 16 **7.** 4 **8.** 11 **9.** 8 **10.** 8 **11.** 7 **12.** 8

PAGE 49

1. $1\frac{1}{2}$ **2.** $1\frac{1}{8}$ **3.** $1\frac{1}{2}$ **4.** $\frac{9}{14}$ **5.** $1\frac{1}{12}$ **6.** $1\frac{1}{20}$ **7.** $\frac{17}{30}$ **8.** $1\frac{1}{24}$ **9.** $1\frac{5}{18}$ **10.** $1\frac{7}{12}$ **11.** $1\frac{2}{15}$ **12.** $\frac{23}{30}$

PAGE 50

1. $\frac{9}{14}$ **2.** $1\frac{1}{10}$ **3.** $1\frac{1}{8}$ **4.** $\frac{5}{6}$ **5.** $\frac{19}{21}$ **6.** $\frac{6}{7}$ **7.** $1\frac{13}{30}$ **8.** $\frac{17}{20}$ **9.** $\frac{11}{12}$ **10.** $\frac{19}{20}$ **11.** $1\frac{1}{15}$ **12.** $\frac{5}{6}$

PAGE 51

1. $\frac{11}{12}$ **2.** $\frac{19}{20}$ **3.** $1\frac{7}{30}$ **4.** $\frac{29}{35}$ **5.** $\frac{13}{21}$ **6.** $\frac{13}{14}$ **7.** $1\frac{3}{10}$ **8.** $\frac{7}{8}$ **9.** $1\frac{1}{6}$ **10.** $1\frac{9}{20}$ **11.** $1\frac{1}{30}$ **12.** $1\frac{19}{30}$

PAGE 52

1. $1\frac{5}{21}$ **2.** $1\frac{6}{35}$ **3.** $\frac{29}{30}$ **4.** $\frac{19}{20}$ **5.** $\frac{7}{12}$ **6.** $1\frac{1}{6}$ **7.** $1\frac{5}{8}$ **8.** $\frac{7}{10}$ **9.** $\frac{13}{14}$ **10.** $\frac{19}{20}$ **11.** $\frac{11}{30}$ **12.** $1\frac{2}{15}$

PAGE 53

1. $\frac{5}{8}$ **2.** $\frac{1}{6}$ **3.** $\frac{2}{15}$ **4.** $\frac{17}{24}$ **5.** $\frac{5}{24}$ **6.** $\frac{2}{15}$ **7.** $\frac{23}{48}$ **8.** $\frac{13}{60}$ **9.** $\frac{5}{21}$ **10.** $\frac{11}{24}$ **11.** $\frac{1}{12}$ **12.** $\frac{9}{64}$

PAGE 54

1. $\frac{1}{9}$ **2.** $\frac{8}{45}$ **3.** $\frac{5}{27}$ **4.** $\frac{3}{20}$ **5.** $\frac{11}{24}$ **6.** $\frac{5}{8}$ **7.** $\frac{1}{2}$ **8.** $\frac{5}{9}$ **9.** $\frac{5}{18}$ **10.** $\frac{11}{15}$ **11.** $\frac{11}{24}$ **12.** $\frac{13}{28}$

Basic Computation Series 2000: Quizzes and Tests
ANSWERS TO EXERCISES

1. $\frac{3}{8}$ 2. $\frac{5}{12}$ 3. $\frac{1}{40}$ 4. $\frac{17}{42}$ 5. $\frac{7}{24}$ 6. $\frac{11}{20}$ 7. $\frac{17}{48}$ 8. $\frac{23}{60}$ 9. $\frac{5}{21}$ 10. $\frac{5}{24}$
11. $\frac{11}{35}$ 12. $\frac{1}{3}$

PAGE 56

1. $\frac{9}{64}$ 2. $\frac{17}{24}$ 3. $\frac{19}{24}$ 4. $\frac{29}{35}$ 5. $\frac{37}{48}$ 6. $\frac{1}{3}$ 7. $\frac{16}{21}$ 8. $\frac{19}{30}$ 9. $\frac{5}{28}$ 10. $\frac{7}{45}$
11. $\frac{53}{75}$ 12. $\frac{1}{6}$

PAGE 57

1. $\frac{11}{75}$ 2. $\frac{6}{11}$ 3. $\frac{1}{4}$ 4. $\frac{1}{2}$ 5. $\frac{9}{31}$ 6. $\frac{6}{35}$ 7. $\frac{519}{850}$ 8. $\frac{50}{729}$ 9. $\frac{1}{30}$ 10. $8\frac{5}{9}$
11. $\frac{5}{26}$ 12. $\frac{1}{11}$

PAGE 58

1. $\frac{1}{80}$ 2. $\frac{1}{63}$ 3. $\frac{4}{25}$ 4. $1\frac{2}{9}$ 5. $\frac{10}{21}$ 6. $\frac{5}{6}$ 7. $\frac{6}{529}$ 8. $4\frac{4}{5}$ 9. $\frac{1}{9}$ 10. $11\frac{1}{4}$
11. $\frac{1}{6}$ 12. $\frac{1}{15}$

PAGE 59

1. $\frac{2}{5}$ 2. $\frac{3}{4}$ 3. $\frac{1}{6}$ 4. $\frac{1}{21}$ 5. $\frac{49}{120}$ 6. $\frac{159}{272}$ 7. $\frac{30}{341}$ 8. $4\frac{1}{3}$ 9. $\frac{1}{4}$ 10. 8
11. 2 12. $2\frac{6}{25}$

PAGE 60

1. $\frac{1}{12}$ 2. $\frac{2}{91}$ 3. $\frac{27}{350}$ 4. $\frac{3}{88}$ 5. $\frac{10}{91}$ 6. $\frac{8}{81}$ 7. $\frac{28}{81}$ 8. $3\frac{5}{9}$ 9. $\frac{8}{135}$
10. 10 11. 52 12. $2\frac{1}{4}$

PAGE 61

1. 4 2. $\frac{11}{12}$ 3. 15 4. $\frac{1}{21}$ 5. 1 6. $\frac{2}{3}$ 7. $1\frac{1}{14}$ 8. $1\frac{3}{4}$ 9. $\frac{3}{104}$ 10. 1
11. 8 12. 32

PAGE 62

1. $\frac{3}{4}$ 2. $\frac{3}{35}$ 3. 7 4. 1 5. $\frac{5}{9}$ 6. $\frac{1}{25}$ 7. $1\frac{4}{5}$ 8. $\frac{1}{28}$ 9. $\frac{4}{5}$ 10. $\frac{7}{16}$ 11. $\frac{2}{7}$
12. $\frac{36}{41}$

PAGE 63

1. $1\frac{2}{3}$ 2. $\frac{2}{9}$ 3. $\frac{1}{2}$ 4. $\frac{32}{99}$ 5. $\frac{7}{22}$ 6. $\frac{3}{40}$ 7. $\frac{20}{27}$ 8. $\frac{1}{24}$ 9. $1\frac{1}{5}$ 10. $\frac{3}{8}$
11. $3\frac{1}{2}$ 12. $\frac{4}{17}$

PAGE 64

1. $\frac{2}{3}$ 2. $1\frac{3}{7}$ 3. $\frac{1}{8}$ 4. 2 5. $5\frac{1}{3}$ 6. $1\frac{1}{15}$ 7. $1\frac{1}{20}$ 8. 10 9. $1\frac{13}{32}$ 10. $\frac{1}{3}$
11. 56 12. $7\frac{1}{2}$

PAGE 65

1. $\frac{22}{39}$ 2. $2\frac{2}{21}$ 3. $1\frac{3}{80}$ 4. $\frac{1}{3}$ 5. $\frac{3}{8}$ 6. $\frac{9}{80}$ 7. $\frac{1}{12}$ 8. $\frac{2}{91}$ 9. $\frac{9}{70}$ 10. $\frac{2}{5}$
11. $1\frac{19}{45}$ 12. $1\frac{17}{63}$

PAGE 66

1. $1\frac{3}{17}$ 2. $1\frac{7}{15}$ 3. $1\frac{3}{80}$ 4. $\frac{1}{20}$ 5. $\frac{11}{24}$ 6. $\frac{9}{32}$ 7. $\frac{3}{88}$ 8. $\frac{2}{21}$ 9. $\frac{8}{81}$
10. $\frac{17}{18}$ 11. $\frac{4}{9}$ 12. $\frac{4}{15}$

PAGE 67

1. $\frac{92}{95}$ 2. $1\frac{31}{48}$ 3. $1\frac{7}{24}$ 4. $\frac{19}{80}$ 5. $\frac{5}{24}$ 6. $\frac{11}{48}$ 7. $\frac{28}{81}$ 8. $\frac{8}{135}$ 9. $3\frac{5}{9}$ 10. $\frac{4}{7}$
11. $11\frac{3}{7}$ 12. $1\frac{1}{6}$

PAGE 68

1. $\frac{8}{9}$ 2. $1\frac{7}{17}$ 3. $\frac{89}{140}$ 4. $\frac{1}{60}$ 5. $\frac{9}{16}$ 6. $\frac{1}{6}$ 7. $\frac{1}{18}$ 8. $\frac{5}{72}$ 9. $\frac{2}{99}$
10. $\frac{3}{4}$ 11. $\frac{9}{55}$ 12. $2\frac{1}{6}$

PAGE 69

1. $13\frac{23}{30}$ 2. $4\frac{5}{6}$ 3. $3\frac{9}{32}$ 4. $16\frac{49}{60}$ 5. $9\frac{7}{12}$ 6. $14\frac{4}{9}$ 7. $12\frac{5}{16}$ 8. $7\frac{3}{10}$
9. $16\frac{3}{4}$ 10. $8\frac{17}{30}$ 11. $16\frac{2}{5}$ 12. $8\frac{3}{14}$

PAGE 70

1. $5\frac{5}{8}$ 2. $20\frac{13}{36}$ 3. $18\frac{3}{8}$ 4. $18\frac{1}{28}$ 5. $10\frac{31}{36}$ 6. $12\frac{19}{20}$ 7. $11\frac{1}{80}$ 8. $19\frac{5}{51}$
9. $16\frac{1}{12}$ 10. $14\frac{9}{10}$ 11. $10\frac{2}{15}$ 12. $12\frac{7}{10}$

PAGE 71

1. $5\frac{7}{40}$ 2. $7\frac{29}{30}$ 3. $11\frac{5}{8}$ 4. $12\frac{5}{16}$ 5. $15\frac{8}{15}$ 6. $10\frac{3}{4}$ 7. $29\frac{25}{48}$ 8. $11\frac{1}{32}$
9. $14\frac{1}{3}$ 10. $13\frac{23}{30}$ 11. $42\frac{11}{30}$ 12. $14\frac{13}{36}$

PAGE 72

1. $16\frac{1}{2}$ 2. $8\frac{5}{8}$ 3. $15\frac{31}{48}$ 4. $6\frac{2}{3}$ 5. $3\frac{4}{5}$ 6. $9\frac{17}{18}$ 7. $25\frac{3}{4}$ 8. $28\frac{29}{40}$
9. $7\frac{3}{100}$ 10. $16\frac{3}{5}$ 11. $4\frac{11}{16}$ 12. $12\frac{4}{15}$

PAGE 73

1. $5\frac{3}{8}$ 2. $20\frac{1}{4}$ 3. $1\frac{1}{2}$ 4. $2\frac{1}{4}$ 5. $8\frac{3}{16}$ 6. $3\frac{9}{16}$ 7. $1\frac{5}{12}$ 8. $2\frac{3}{8}$ 9. $2\frac{1}{16}$
10. 35 11. $8\frac{23}{40}$ 12. $3\frac{1}{6}$

PAGE 74

1. $6\frac{17}{48}$ 2. $7\frac{5}{8}$ 3. $6\frac{5}{16}$ 4. $3\frac{5}{6}$ 5. $5\frac{1}{8}$ 6. $2\frac{5}{16}$ 7. $1\frac{4}{15}$ 8. $5\frac{29}{32}$ 9. $2\frac{3}{8}$
10. $2\frac{23}{30}$ 11. $3\frac{5}{12}$ 12. $8\frac{1}{6}$

PAGE 75

1. $\frac{1}{4}$ 2. $2\frac{7}{20}$ 3. $10\frac{1}{8}$ 4. $7\frac{7}{8}$ 5. $9\frac{7}{36}$ 6. $1\frac{11}{12}$ 7. $\frac{3}{8}$ 8. $3\frac{13}{20}$ 9. $2\frac{9}{28}$
10. $1\frac{7}{12}$ 11. $2\frac{3}{4}$ 12. $5\frac{1}{10}$

PAGE 76

1. $13\frac{2}{15}$ 2. $34\frac{5}{6}$ 3. $7\frac{1}{16}$ 4. $\frac{23}{40}$ 5. $5\frac{3}{14}$ 6. $\frac{5}{16}$ 7. $1\frac{1}{15}$ 8. $3\frac{11}{24}$
9. $11\frac{7}{8}$ 10. $19\frac{3}{4}$ 11. $1\frac{7}{8}$ 12. $3\frac{1}{6}$

PAGE 77

1. $13\frac{13}{15}$ 2. 20 3. 6 4. $16\frac{1}{24}$ 5. $6\frac{1}{4}$ 6. $56\frac{1}{4}$ 7. 33 8. $7\frac{6}{7}$
9. 35 10. 21 11. $72\frac{25}{48}$ 12. 35

PAGE 78

1. $7\frac{1}{5}$ 2. $9\frac{7}{12}$ 3. 18 4. 24 5. $41\frac{1}{7}$ 6. $81\frac{2}{3}$ 7. $10\frac{1}{16}$ 8. $36\frac{2}{3}$
9. $23\frac{1}{5}$ 10. 8 11. 8 12. $\frac{1}{2}$

PAGE 79

1. $42\frac{1}{2}$ **2.** 6 **3.** $26\frac{23}{48}$ **4.** 16 **5.** $2\frac{2}{3}$ **6.** 6 **7.** 35 **8.** 21
9. 60 **10.** $22\frac{1}{2}$ **11.** $9\frac{7}{9}$ **12.** 24

PAGE 80

1. $9\frac{1}{15}$ **2.** 65 **3.** 16 **4.** 18 **5.** $4\frac{2}{3}$ **6.** 12 **7.** $2\frac{2}{3}$ **8.** 63 **9.** $104\frac{1}{6}$
10. 4 **11.** 51 **12.** 27

PAGE 81

1. $\frac{24}{49}$ **2.** $2\frac{1}{2}$ **3.** $2\frac{3}{5}$ **4.** 20 **5.** $1\frac{1}{5}$ **6.** $\frac{25}{54}$ **7.** 7 **8.** $1\frac{1}{4}$ **9.** $\frac{5}{7}$ **10.** 2
11. 6 **12.** $\frac{52}{77}$

PAGE 82

1. $\frac{3}{4}$ **2.** $\frac{2}{3}$ **3.** $\frac{6}{7}$ **4.** $8\frac{1}{5}$ **5.** 2 **6.** 4 **7.** $1\frac{7}{18}$ **8.** $2\frac{1}{2}$ **9.** 8 **10.** $\frac{56}{75}$
11. $2\frac{33}{50}$ **12.** $\frac{2}{5}$

PAGE 83

1. $1\frac{1}{5}$ **2.** $1\frac{1}{3}$ **3.** $\frac{40}{63}$ **4.** 2 **5.** $1\frac{8}{27}$ **6.** $1\frac{25}{52}$ **7.** $\frac{1}{6}$ **8.** 1 **9.** 3 **10.** $\frac{18}{49}$
11. $1\frac{3}{4}$ **12.** $\frac{15}{58}$

PAGE 84

1. $\frac{1}{6}$ **2.** 2 **3.** 4 **4.** $4\frac{1}{5}$ **5.** $2\frac{1}{7}$ **6.** $1\frac{1}{3}$ **7.** $\frac{1}{2}$ **8.** $\frac{1}{4}$ **9.** $2\frac{2}{9}$ **10.** $4\frac{10}{11}$
11. $1\frac{25}{26}$ **12.** $3\frac{1}{2}$

PAGE 85

1. $6\frac{3}{8}$ **2.** $7\frac{1}{3}$ **3.** $17\frac{1}{16}$ **4.** $4\frac{1}{2}$ **5.** $5\frac{1}{6}$ **6.** $6\frac{1}{2}$ **7.** 111 **8.** 27 **9.** 25
10. $1\frac{1}{7}$ **11.** 24 **12.** $3\frac{1}{16}$

PAGE 86

1. $42\frac{21}{40}$ **2.** $15\frac{11}{24}$ **3.** $10\frac{13}{30}$ **4.** $18\frac{19}{24}$ **5.** $3\frac{7}{16}$ **6.** $6\frac{37}{80}$ **7.** $6\frac{3}{10}$ **8.** $5\frac{1}{32}$
9. $31\frac{1}{2}$ **10.** $2\frac{32}{33}$ **11.** 4 **12.** $1\frac{1}{2}$

PAGE 87

1. $48\frac{5}{36}$ **2.** $74\frac{35}{48}$ **3.** $12\frac{43}{60}$ **4.** $5\frac{5}{6}$ **5.** $5\frac{43}{48}$ **6.** $24\frac{13}{20}$ **7.** $11\frac{1}{2}$ **8.** $4\frac{3}{8}$
9. $22\frac{3}{4}$ **10.** $\frac{75}{88}$ **11.** 20 **12.** $\frac{5}{8}$

PAGE 88

1. $19\frac{4}{9}$ **2.** $32\frac{9}{16}$ **3.** $23\frac{11}{24}$ **4.** $12\frac{11}{35}$ **5.** $5\frac{7}{12}$ **6.** $8\frac{11}{24}$ **7.** 5 **8.** $8\frac{7}{10}$
9. $7\frac{1}{5}$ **10.** 7 **11.** $\frac{6}{7}$ **12.** $1\frac{19}{33}$

PAGE 89

1. $49\frac{3}{4}$ **2.** $73\frac{1}{2}$ miles **3.** $2\frac{1}{4}$ in. **4.** $1\frac{23}{24}$ miles **5.** $1\frac{1}{4}$
6. $2\frac{2}{3}$ **7.** 22 **8.** $5\frac{1}{2}$ ft

PAGE 90

1. $127\frac{31}{48}$ **2.** $13\frac{3}{4}$ **3.** $1\frac{3}{8}$ **4.** $\frac{5}{8}$ **5.** $\frac{3}{4}$ mile **6.** $1\frac{25}{32}$ miles
7. $30\frac{1}{2}$ **8.** $1\frac{4}{9}$ ft

PAGE 91

1. $60\frac{7}{8}$ miles **2.** $12\frac{7}{8}$ **3.** $1\frac{7}{8}$ in. **4.** $\frac{9}{16}$ mile **5.** $\frac{13}{14}$ **6.** $13\frac{1}{2}$ cups
7. $31\frac{1}{2}$ **8.** $1\frac{5}{6}$ yd

PAGE 92

1. $128\frac{1}{8}$ **2.** $575\frac{7}{16}$ lb; no **3.** $\frac{5}{8}$ **4.** $1\frac{5}{8}$ ft **5.** $\frac{7}{8}$ mile
6. $2\frac{1}{4}$ cups **7.** $51\frac{1}{5}$ **8.** $1\frac{11}{20}$ yd

PAGE 93

1. three thousand two hundred seventeen **2.** forty-three and eight hundred twenty-one thousandths **3.** 70,055 **4.** 300.122 **5.** $0.\overline{3}$
6. 0.625 **7.** $\frac{11}{25}$ **8.** $\frac{173}{200}$ **9.** 3,800 **10.** 56.44 **11.** 63,000 **12.** 434.2

PAGE 94

1. four thousand three hundred seventy-nine **2.** four hundred seventy-six and eighty-three thousandths **3.** 894,026 **4.** 622.37
5. $0.\overline{27}$ **6.** 0.875 **7.** $\frac{17}{25}$ **8.** $\frac{381}{500}$ **9.** 8,600 **10.** 68.64 **11.** 890,000
12. 11.4

PAGE 95

1. fifty-nine thousand six hundred forty-seven **2.** eight thousand six hundred seventy-four and ninety-three hundredths **3.** 97,066
4. 202.098 **5.** $0.\overline{714285}$ **6.** $0.8\overline{3}$ **7.** $\frac{47}{50}$ **8.** $\frac{153}{200}$ **9.** 55,000
10. 543.8 **11.** 8,000 **12.** 474

PAGE 96

1. nine thousand eight hundred sixty-four **2.** five hundred seventy-four and eight hundred seven thousandths **3.** 9,602.08
4. 500,000.005 **5.** $0.\overline{8}$ **6.** 0.9375 **7.** $\frac{8}{25}$ **8.** $\frac{3}{8}$ **9.** 98.4 **10.** 650
11. 800 **12.** 89.44

PAGE 97

1. 72.3 **2.** 1.007 **3.** 82.371 **4.** 27.887 **5.** 70.246 **6.** 23.6782
7. 64.385 **8.** 34.8607 **9.** 268.6884 **10.** 198.5021 **11.** 363.88
12. 382.702

PAGE 98

1. 46 **2.** 1.3989 **3.** 163.9987 **4.** 29.6526 **5.** 51.026 **6.** 83.6759
7. 70.893 **8.** 104.3906 **9.** 195.5999 **10.** 187.1496 **11.** 66.56
12. 552.131

PAGE 99

1. 12.4 **2.** 1.3874 **3.** 150.15 **4.** 23.003 **5.** 65.036 **6.** 42.9993
7. 50.88 **8.** 10.8205 **9.** 280.7317 **10.** 168.2426 **11.** 74.84
12. 358.03

PAGE 100

1. 142.95 **2.** 0.00012 **3.** 58.3 **4.** 551.694 **5.** 102.12 **6.** 539.91
7. 597.3 **8.** 100.626 **9.** 203.124 **10.** 193.392 **11.** 13.207
12. 69.7462

PAGE 101
1. 8,788.35 **2.** 857.44 **3.** 197.927 **4.** 755.6 **5.** 27.8803
6. 19.029 **7.** 2,412.37 **8.** 153.982 **9.** 1,816.25 **10.** 79.685
11. 8.922 **12.** 2,938.23

PAGE 102
1. 45.02473 **2.** 0.132818 **3.** 74.786 **4.** 79.86995 **5.** 6.5428
6. 20.6712 **7.** 274.975 **8.** 27.89379 **9.** 47.77 **10.** 1.0478
11. 32.4761 **12.** 152.7065

PAGE 103
1. 185.69 **2.** 45.096 **3.** 0.52685 **4.** 100.617 **5.** 32,297.037
6. 1.5788 **7.** 28.726 **8.** 20.3348 **9.** 35.562 **10.** 233.544
11. 1,490.784 **12.** 13,401.507

PAGE 104
1. 7,588.27 **2.** 380.98 **3.** 169.965 **4.** 867.8 **5.** 39.8608 **6.** 4.079
7. 1,123.07 **8.** 130.975 **9.** 1,415.17 **10.** 7.311 **11.** 2,610.13
12. 42,022.221

PAGE 105
1. 15.078 **2.** 100.45 **3.** 0.11418 **4.** 594 **5.** 5.0662 **6.** 35.14
7. 678.6 **8.** 3.492 **9.** 44.4577 **10.** 352.88 **11.** 0.168
12. 4,282.18

PAGE 106
1. 10.191 **2.** 157.92 **3.** 0.07612 **4.** 680.36 **5.** 3.8761
6. 15.96672 **7.** 73.47 **8.** 1.416 **9.** 6.0576 **10.** 298.98
11. 0.3995 **12.** 3.78176

PAGE 107
1. 22.512 **2.** 13.832 **3.** 0.136032 **4.** 2,086 **5.** 1.61393
6. 17.1174 **7.** 748.8 **8.** 466.52 **9.** 19.8288 **10.** 1,079.5
11. 0.21162 **12.** 3,650

PAGE 108
1. 17.064 **2.** 18.3114 **3.** 152.5533 **4.** 9,391.36 **5.** 28.8123
6. 847.705 **7.** 600.502 **8.** 2,062.83 **9.** 97.137 **10.** 26.767
11. 0.0243872 **12.** 408.58

PAGE 109
1. 0.0902 **2.** 62.57 **3.** 15.36 **4.** 0.125 **5.** 0.13747 **6.** 14.5
7. 8.72 **8.** 440 **9.** 0.4375 **10.** 15.8 **11.** 1.654 **12.** 15.63

PAGE 110
1. 0.0601 **2.** 2.31 **3.** 6.541 **4.** 0.375 **5.** 0.13679 **6.** 25.7
7. 65.41 **8.** 120 **9.** 0.3125 **10.** 12.67 **11.** 0.1739 **12.** 17.83

PAGE 111
1. 0.0701 **2.** 39.5 **3.** 7.94 **4.** 0.875 **5.** 0.07787 **6.** 10.8 **7.** 46.5
8. 160 **9.** 0.5625 **10.** 53.6 **11.** 0.804 **12.** 387.5

PAGE 112
1. 0.068 **2.** 40.6 **3.** 10.203 **4.** 0.625 **5.** 200.1 **6.** 16,717 **7.** 205
8. 200 **9.** 0.6875 **10.** 910.04 **11.** 834 **12.** 400

PAGE 113
1. 9,666.83 **2.** 1,156.6756 **3.** 900.733 **4.** 375.919 **5.** 823.89
6. 838.703 **7.** 6.491394 **8.** 11.02864 **9.** 212.861 **10.** 9.55
11. 2.011 **12.** 91.2

PAGE 114
1. 820.4839 **2.** 510.3823 **3.** 198.17 **4.** 22.6939 **5.** 455.37
6. 709.039 **7.** 17.8608 **8.** 121.7872 **9.** 64.1586 **10.** 6.45
11. 3.012 **12.** 65.4

PAGE 115
1. 49.3875 **2.** 879.909 **3.** 7,151.23 **4.** 677.882 **5.** 2.885
6. 688.405 **7.** 8.8395 **8.** 58.443 **9.** 833.4128 **10.** 7.12
11. 2.001 **12.** 76.2

PAGE 116
1. 62.3843 **2.** 998.076 **3.** 1,085.825 **4.** 878.341 **5.** 31.102
6. 782.168 **7.** 10.205 **8.** 3,715.35 **9.** 761.392 **10.** 8.15
11. 1.059 **12.** 83.2

PAGE 117
1. $620.26 **2.** $8,515.20 **3.** 100,000 **4.** $13,288.71
5. 11,894.217 **6.** 4.02 in. **7.** 2,898 cm³ **8.** $3,013.85

PAGE 118
1. 7.48 **2.** $379.72 **3.** 131.25 cups **4.** 22.67 **5.** 13,095.015 miles
6. $1,450.68 **7.** 9.8 lb **8.** 8.5

PAGE 119
1. $97.34 **2.** $1,900.81 **3.** $467.46 **4.** 741 people
5. 3,684.79 cm³ **6.** 7,584.752 **7.** 73.78 miles **8.** 1.46 mi²

PAGE 120
1. $298.65 **2.** $5.55 **3.** $2,891.89 **4.** $144.35 **5.** $3,386.90
6. 560.56 miles **7.** 12.13 miles **8.** 0.007 mi²

PAGE 121
1. 80% **2.** 50% **3.** 62% **4.** 0.4% **5.** 62.5% **6.** 13.86 **7.** 0.052
8. 76 **9.** $\frac{18}{25}$ **10.** 33 **11.** 6.48 **12.** $66\frac{2}{3}$%

PAGE 122
1. 3.5% **2.** 10.88 **3.** 0.31% **4.** 75% **5.** $\frac{21}{25}$ **6.** 1.472 **7.** 87.5%
8. 120% **9.** 57% **10.** 60 **11.** 1,750% **12.** 37.5%

PAGE 123
1. 40% **2.** 0.0016 **3.** 80% **4.** 10.71 **5.** 0.51% **6.** 24 **7.** 108
8. 40% **9.** 13 **10.** 20% **11.** 76% **12.** 25%

PAGE 124
1. 25% **2.** 29% **3.** 0.43 **4.** 30% **5.** 20% **6.** 5.25 **7.** 27
8. 63 **9.** 20% **10.** 18% **11.** 6.396 **12.** 20%

PAGE 125
1. 27 **2.** 83 **3.** 16% **4.** $198 **5.** 30% **6.** $450 **7.** $30
8. $1,000 **9.** $120 **10.** $56,000

PAGE 126
1. 62 **2.** 87 **3.** 42% **4.** $196 **5.** $300 **6.** 20% **7.** $40
8. $1,500 **9.** $135 **10.** $84,750

1. 33 **2.** 72 **3.** 45% **4.** $336 **5.** $12\frac{1}{2}$% **6.** $42 **7.** $288

8. $2,200 **9.** $108 **10.** $94,500

PAGE 128

1. 64 **2.** 103 **3.** 51% **4.** $225 **5.** $33\frac{1}{3}$% **6.** $473 **7.** $56

8. $2,000 **9.** $131.25 **10.** $103,500

PAGE 129

1. 113 **2.** 35 **3.** 194 **4.** 240 **5.** 6 **6.** 60 **7.** 18 **8.** 45 **9.** 540
10. 1,400 **11.** 3,520 **12.** 204

PAGE 130

1. 68 **2.** 25 **3.** 176 **4.** 84 **5.** 17 **6.** 16 **7.** 4,700 **8.** 26,000
9. 30.1 **10.** 32,000 **11.** 5.20 **12.** 0.017

PAGE 131

1. 95 **2.** 60 **3.** 122 **4.** 11 **5.** 300 **6.** 144 **7.** 52 **8.** 15,840
9. 1,236 **10.** 14 **11.** 141 **12.** 5,280

PAGE 132

1. 140 **2.** 50 **3.** 65 **4.** 15 **5.** 52 **6.** 15 **7.** 47,000 **8.** 6.152
9. 0.00083 **10.** 5.9 **11.** 0.0635 **12.** 0.082

PAGE 133

1. 120° **2.** 49° **3.** 47°, 63°, 70° **4.** 36°, 100°, 44°
5. 60°, 100°, 110°, 90° **6.** 53°, 60°, 67°

PAGE 134

1. 122° **2.** 70° **3.** 52°, 88°, 40° **4.** 90°, 32°, 58°
5. 44°, 105°, 31° **6.** 88°, 77°, 80°, 115°

PAGE 135

1. 60° **2.** 105° **3.** 55°, 75°, 50° **4.** 43°, 90°, 47°
5. 80°, 86°, 106°, 88° **6.** 22°, 141°, 17°

PAGE 136

1. 137° **2.** 70° **3.** 68°, 30°, 82° **4.** 27°, 103°, 50°
5. 48°, 81°, 51° **6.** 89°, 83°, 88°, 100°

PAGE 137

1. $3\frac{1}{8}$ in.^{2}, $7\frac{1}{2}$ in. **2.** 2 yd^2, 6 yd **3.** 5 ft^2, 9 ft **4.** $12\frac{1}{4}$ in.^{2}, 14 in.
5. $2\frac{13}{16}$ mi^2, 7 mi

PAGE 138

1. 3.75 m^2, 8 m **2.** 2.25 km^2, 6.5 km **3.** 3.0625 dm^2, 7 dm

4. 5.3125 m^2, 11 m **5.** 7.875 cm^2, 13.5 cm

PAGE 139

1. $6\frac{7}{8}$ in.^{2}, $13\frac{1}{2}$ in. **2.** $5\frac{1}{2}$ mi^2, $9\frac{1}{2}$ mi **3.** $4\frac{1}{2}$ ft^2, 9 ft
4. $4\frac{7}{8}$ yd^2, $9\frac{1}{2}$ yd **5.** 3 in.^{2}, $9\frac{1}{2}$ in.

PAGE 140 |

1. 4.375 km^2, 8.5 km **2.** 2.5 dm^2, 6.5 dm **3.** 8.4375 m^2, 12 m
4. 3.5 km^2, 7.8 km **5.** 4.25 cm^2, 10.5 cm

PAGE 141

1. $1\frac{1}{4}$ in., 3 in., $3\frac{1}{4}$ in., $1\frac{1}{4}$ in., $1\frac{7}{8}$ in.^{2}, $7\frac{1}{2}$ in.

2. $1\frac{3}{4}$ in., $3\frac{1}{2}$ in., 2 in., $1\frac{3}{4}$ in., $1\frac{1}{2}$ in., $4\frac{1}{8}$ in.^{2}, 9 in.

3. $1\frac{1}{2}$ in., $2\frac{1}{2}$ in., $1\frac{1}{2}$ in., $3\frac{3}{4}$ in.^{2}, 8 in.

PAGE 142

1. 41 mm, 51 mm, 48 mm, 36 mm, 918 mm^2, 140 mm
2. 39 mm, 70 mm, 38 mm, 2,660 mm^2, 218 mm
3. 43 mm, 72 mm, 45 mm, 48 mm, 43 mm, 2,515.5 mm^2, 208 mm

PAGE 143

1. $1\frac{1}{4}$ in., $3\frac{3}{4}$ in., $1\frac{1}{4}$ in., $4\frac{11}{16}$ in.^{2}, 10 in.
2. $2\frac{1}{2}$ in., $3\frac{1}{2}$ in., 2 in., $1\frac{1}{2}$ in., $2\frac{5}{8}$ in.^{2}, 8 in.
3. 2 in., $4\frac{1}{4}$ in., 2 in., 2 in., $1\frac{3}{4}$ in., $5\frac{15}{32}$ in.^{2}, $10\frac{1}{4}$ in.

PAGE 144

1. 43 mm, 90 mm, 68 mm, 32 mm, 1,440 mm^2, 201 mm
2. 39 mm, 59 mm, 38 mm, 2,242 mm^2, 196 mm
3. 40 mm, 77 mm, 51 mm, 44 mm, 39 mm, 2,496 mm^2, 212 mm

PAGE 145

1. 294 in.^{2}, 343 in.^{3} **2.** 1,942 ft^2, 5,525 ft^3 **3.** 12,170.64 in.^{2},
58,944.08 in.^{3} **4.** 325 in.^{3} **5.** 381,510 ft^3 **6.** 2,001,750 in.^{3}

PAGE 146

1. 1,014 cm^2, 2,197 cm^3 **2.** 572 mm^2, 816 mm^3 **3.** 2,285.92 cm^2,
7,385.28 cm^3 **4.** 1,140 cm^3 **5.** 38,772.72 m^3 **6.** 10,562.96 mm^3

PAGE 147

1. 726 in.^{2}, 1,331 in.^{3} **2.** 438 ft^2, 432 ft^3 **3.** 18,463.2 yd^2,
155,090.88 yd^3 **4.** 10,500 in.^{3} **5.** 179,503.$\overline{3}$ in.^{3} **6.** 67,852.26 in.^{3}

PAGE 148

1. 384 mm^2, 512 mm^3 **2.** 2,452 cm^2, 6,160 cm^3 **3.** 6,506.08 cm^2,
22,155.84 cm^3 **4.** 539 m^3 **5.** 113,040 cm^3 **6.** 4,019.2 m^3

PAGE 149

1. 25 in., 157 in., 1,962.5 in.^{2} **2.** 19 ft, 119.32 ft, 1,133.54 ft^2
3. 2 yd, 12.56 yd, 12.56 yd^2 **4.** 15 ft, 94.2 ft, 706.5 ft^2
5. 7.5 in., 47.1 in., 176.625 in.^{2}

PAGE 150

1. 17 mm, 106.76 mm, 907.46 mm^2 **2.** 20 cm, 125.6 cm, 1,256 cm^2
3. 10 dm, 62.8 dm, 314 dm^2 **4.** 18 m, 113.04 m, 1,017.36 m^2
5. 9.5 cm, 59.66 cm, 283.385 cm^2

PAGE 151

1. 5 yd, 31.4 yd, 78.5 yd^2 **2.** 16 in., 100.48 in., 803.84 in.^{2}
3. 9 ft, 56.52 ft, 254.34 ft^2 **4.** 26 in., 163.28 in., 2,122.64 in.^{2}
5. 22.5 ft, 141.3 ft, 1,589.625 ft^2

PAGE 152

1. 2.5 km, 15.7 km, 19.625 km^2 **2.** 30 mm, 188.4 mm, 2,826 mm^2
3. 7 dm, 43.96 dm, 153.86 dm^2 **4.** 38 cm, 238.64 cm, 4,534.16 cm^2
5. 12.5 m, 78.5 m, 490.625 m^2

PAGE 153

1. 1 $10, 1 25¢, 3 1¢ **2.** 3 $1, 1 10¢, 1 5¢, 4 1¢ **3.** 1 $5, 2 $1, 1 25¢, 1 10¢, 1 5¢, 3 1¢ **4.** 1 $10, 1 $1, 2 25¢, 1 10¢, 1 5¢, 3 1¢ **5.** 1 $10, 4 $1, 3 25¢, 1 5¢, 4 1¢ **6.** 1 $10, 2 $1, 2 10¢, 2 1¢ **7.** c **8.** c **9.** b **10.** a **11.** c **12.** c

PAGE 154

1. 1 $10, 2 $1, 2 25¢, 1 10¢, 1 5¢, 3 1¢ **2.** 4 $1, 1 25¢, 1 10¢, 1 5¢, 3 1¢ **3.** 1 $5, 2 $1, 1 25¢, 1 10¢, 1 5¢, 1 1¢ **4.** 1 $10, 1 $5,1 $1, 1 25¢, 1 5¢, 2 1¢ **5.** 1 $10, 1 10¢, 1 5¢, 2 1¢ **6.** 1 $10, 2 $1, 3 1¢ **7.** b **8.** c **9.** a **10.** a **11.** c **12.** b

PAGE 155

1. 1 $5, 2 $1, 2 25¢, 1 1¢ **2.** 1 10$, 2 $1, 1 10¢, 1 5¢, 2 1¢ **3.** 3 $1, 2 25¢, 2 1¢ **4.** 1 $10, 1 $5, 3 25¢, 1 10¢, 1 5¢, 3 1¢ **5.** 1 $10, 1 $1, 1 25¢, 2 10¢, 3 1¢ **6.** 1 $5, 1 10¢, 1 5¢, 4 1¢ **7.** a **8.** c **9.** c **10.** c **11.** b **12.** a

PAGE 156

1. 1 $5, 3 $ 1, 1 25¢, 1 10¢, 1 5¢, 2 1¢ **2.** 1 $5, 1 $1, 2 25¢, 1 10¢, 1 5¢, 3 1¢ **3.** 2 $1, 1 10¢, 1 5¢, 3 1¢ **4.** 1 $10, 2 25¢, 2 10¢, 2 1¢ **5.** 1 $10, 2 $1, 1 10¢, 1 5¢ **6.** 1 $10, 1 25¢, 1 10¢, 4 1¢ **7.** b **8.** a **9.** c **10.** c **11.** b **12.** c

PAGE 157

1. 12% **2.** 288 **3.** $102\frac{2}{3}$ **4.** 6,803 ft **5.** $2.23 **6.** 13.9 mi/hr

PAGE 158

1. 49% **2.** 51 **3.** $178.92 **4.** $126.75 **5.** $109,949 **6.** $198

PAGE 159

1. 3.08 sec **2.** 1.6 km/hr **3.** 114 **4.** 14% **5.** $11.13 **6.** $36,117.25

PAGE 160

1. 80.2 **2.** $337.12 **3.** $70.08 **4.** $625 **5.** $58 **6.** $0.05

PAGES 161–173

1. C **2.** A **3.** A **4.** C **5.** A **6.** A **7.** D **8.** B **9.** D **10.** B
11. C **12.** D **13.** B **14.** D **15.** A **16.** A **17.** B **18.** D **19.** C **20.** C
21. A **22.** B **23.** D **24.** D **25.** C **26.** B **27.** C **28.** B **29.** B **30.** D
31. C **32.** D **33.** C **34.** D **35.** C **36.** D **37.** A **38.** D **39.** A **40.** B
41. A **42.** D **43.** B **44.** A **45.** D **46.** D **47.** D **48.** A **49.** B **50.** C
51. B **52.** B **53.** B **54.** C **55.** A **56.** D **57.** C **58.** B **59.** B **60.** D
61. C **62.** C **63.** D **64.** A **65.** A **66.** A **67.** B **68.** C **69.** A **70.** B
71. B **72.** D **73.** C **74.** C **75.** D **76.** C **77.** A **78.** B **79.** A **80.** A
81. C **82.** C **83.** B **84.** B **85.** A **86.** B **87.** A **88.** C **89.** D **90.** B
91. A **92.** A **93.** A **94.** B **95.** C **96.** D **97.** C **98.** B **99.** D
100. C

PAGES 174–186

1. C **2.** A **3.** C **4.** A **5.** A **6.** B **7.** C **8.** A **9.** D **10.** D
11. B **12.** D **13.** C **14.** A **15.** B **16.** C **17.** C **18.** B **19.** A **20.** D
21. A **22.** D **23.** D **24.** B **25.** B **26.** C **27.** D **28.** A **29.** C **30.** D
31. D **32.** D **33.** C **34.** B **35.** D **36.** A **37.** C **38.** A **39.** A **40.** C
41. D **42.** B **43.** B **44.** A **45.** D **46.** B **47.** C **48.** D **49.** B **50.** A
51. B **52.** B **53.** C **54.** D **55.** C **56.** B **57.** B **58.** C **59.** A **60.** B
61. C **62.** D **63.** D **64.** C **65.** D **66.** B **67.** D **68.** A **69.** A **70.** B
71. C **72.** B **73.** A **74.** A **75.** C **76.** A **77.** B **78.** D **79.** B **80.** D
81. A **82.** B **83.** A **84.** C **85.** C **86.** D **87.** C **88.** B **89.** D **90.** C
91. A **92.** D **93.** A **94.** B **95.** D **96.** A **97.** A **98.** B **99.** C
100. C

PAGES 187–199

1. D **2.** A **3.** B **4.** C **5.** A **6.** B **7.** A **8.** C **9.** D **10.** B
11. D **12.** D **13.** A **14.** C **15.** B **16.** A **17.** A **18.** C **19.** A **20.** C
21. C **22.** A **23.** A **24.** C **25.** A **26.** D **27.** B **28.** C **29.** D **30.** D
31. D **32.** C **33.** A **34.** D **35.** C **36.** B **37.** B **38.** D **39.** D **40.** A
41. B **42.** A **43.** C **44.** B **45.** B **46.** C **47.** B **48.** C **49.** D **50.** B
51. A **52.** B **53.** D **54.** C **55.** B **56.** D **57.** A **58.** B **59.** B **60.** D
61. D **62.** B **63.** D **64.** B **65.** A **66.** C **67.** A **68.** C **69.** B **70.** C
71. B **72.** A **73.** A **74.** B **75.** C **76.** D **77.** D **78.** D **79.** D **80.** C
81. C **82.** C **83.** B **84.** A **85.** A **86.** D **87.** B **88.** A **89.** D **90.** A
91. C **92.** D **93.** B **94.** C **95.** D **96.** C **97.** C **98.** A **99.** B
100. A

PAGES 200–212

1. D **2.** C **3.** B **4.** D **5.** C **6.** A **7.** A **8.** A **9.** B **10.** A
11. B **12.** A **13.** C **14.** D **15.** B **16.** C **17.** C **18.** B **19.** B **20.** A
21. C **22.** A **23.** C **24.** A **25.** A **26.** B **27.** D **28.** C **29.** C **30.** D
31. A **32.** B **33.** B **34.** A **35.** B **36.** C **37.** C **38.** C **39.** A **40.** A
41. D **42.** D **43.** D **44.** B **45.** D **46.** B **47.** D **48.** B **49.** C **50.** A
51. D **52.** D **53.** A **54.** B **55.** C **56.** D **57.** C **58.** B **59.** A **60.** D
61. A **62.** A **63.** D **64.** A **65.** B **66.** C **67.** D **68.** C **69.** B **70.** C
71. B **72.** C **73.** B **74.** C **75.** A **76.** D **77.** B **78.** D **79.** D **80.** C
81. A **82.** B **83.** A **84.** D **85.** C **86.** C **87.** D **88.** B **89.** D **90.** A
91. A **92.** D **93.** B **94.** B **95.** D **96.** C **97.** A **98.** D **99.** C
100. A

Response Form

1.	A	B	C	D	26.	A	B	C	D	51.	A	B	C	D	76.	A	B	C	D
2.	A	B	C	D	27.	A	B	C	D	52.	A	B	C	D	77.	A	B	C	D
3.	A	B	C	D	28.	A	B	C	D	53.	A	B	C	D	78.	A	B	C	D
4.	A	B	C	D	29.	A	B	C	D	54.	A	B	C	D	79.	A	B	C	D
5.	A	B	C	D	30.	A	B	C	D	55.	A	B	C	D	80.	A	B	C	D
6.	A	B	C	D	31.	A	B	C	D	56.	A	B	C	D	81.	A	B	C	D
7.	A	B	C	D	32.	A	B	C	D	57.	A	B	C	D	82.	A	B	C	D
8.	A	B	C	D	33.	A	B	C	D	58.	A	B	C	D	83.	A	B	C	D
9.	A	B	C	D	34.	A	B	C	D	59.	A	B	C	D	84.	A	B	C	D
10.	A	B	C	D	35.	A	B	C	D	60.	A	B	C	D	85.	A	B	C	D
11.	A	B	C	D	36.	A	B	C	D	61.	A	B	C	D	86.	A	B	C	D
12.	A	B	C	D	37.	A	B	C	D	62.	A	B	C	D	87.	A	B	C	D
13.	A	B	C	D	38.	A	B	C	D	63.	A	B	C	D	88.	A	B	C	D
14.	A	B	C	D	39.	A	B	C	D	64.	A	B	C	D	89.	A	B	C	D
15.	A	B	C	D	40.	A	B	C	D	65.	A	B	C	D	90.	A	B	C	D
16.	A	B	C	D	41.	A	B	C	D	66.	A	B	C	D	91.	A	B	C	D
17.	A	B	C	D	42.	A	B	C	D	67.	A	B	C	D	92.	A	B	C	D
18.	A	B	C	D	43.	A	B	C	D	68.	A	B	C	D	93.	A	B	C	D
19.	A	B	C	D	44.	A	B	C	D	69.	A	B	C	D	94.	A	B	C	D
20.	A	B	C	D	45.	A	B	C	D	70.	A	B	C	D	95.	A	B	C	D
21.	A	B	C	D	46.	A	B	C	D	71.	A	B	C	D	96.	A	B	C	D
22.	A	B	C	D	47.	A	B	C	D	72.	A	B	C	D	97.	A	B	C	D
23.	A	B	C	D	48.	A	B	C	D	73.	A	B	C	D	98.	A	B	C	D
24.	A	B	C	D	49.	A	B	C	D	74.	A	B	C	D	99.	A	B	C	D
25.	A	B	C	D	50.	A	B	C	D	75.	A	B	C	D	100.	A	B	C	D

Basic Computation Series 2000: Quizzes and Tests
RESPONSE FORM